The Biblical Doctrine

of

Election and Predestination

The Biblical Doctrine
of
Election and Predestination

Why a Baptist will never hold to a doctrine
of Calvinism or Augustinian Predestination

by

Pastor Edward G. Rice

Pastor E. G. Rice Publications
Good Samaritan Baptist Church
54 Main St. Box 99, Dresden NY 14441
www.GSBaptistChurch.com
Phone: (315) 536-0878   Email: PastorRice@GSBaptistChurch.com

Cover Design by Author
Copy Right Info on Cover Pictures
Image: Portrait of Calvin, John. 1509-1564, Source : Hundred Greatest Men, The. New York: D. Appleton & Company, 1885.,Public domain: This image is in the public domain because its copyright has expired. www.lib.utexas.edu

Image:Augustine of Hippo.jpg, Original source: Hundred Greatest Men, The. New York: D. Appleton & Company, 1885. Public domain This image is in the public domain because its copyright has expired. www.lib.utexas.edu

Image:Sainte Monique.jpg, Permission - Public domain, The two-dimensional work of art depicted in this image is in the public domain worldwide due to the date of death of its author Therefore this photographical reproduction is also in the public domain.

Image:Tiffany Window of St Augustine - Lightner Museum.jpg, Tiffany stained-glass window of St. Augustine, in the Lightner Museum, St. Augustine, Creator Name: Tiffany, Louis Comfort,Date of birth: 1848-02-18,Location of birth: New York, New York, Date of death: 1933-01-17, Location of death: New York, New York,Public domain, since artist died more than 70 years ago.

Image: Frayed Tulip Taken by author.

Image: Pastel of Closed Tulip, commissioned by author from Valarie Poorman

Printed and bound in the United States by LuLu.com
Published by Pastor E. G. Rice Publishing
54 Main St. Box 99
Dresden NY 14441

ISBN: 978-0-578-02455-4

Library of Congress No.

206XXXXXXX

Dedication

"The author who benefits you most is not the one who tells you something you did not know before, but the one who gives expression to the truth that has been dumbly struggling in you for utterance.[1]" The author who benefited me most concerning the errors of Calvinism was without doubt Samuel Fisk in his book "Calvinistic Paths Retraced." Fisk's editor describes the work with three words: Scriptural, Scholarship, and Thoroughness. Having spent 30 years bumping into the ugly doctrine of Calvinism in Baptist Churches, I found that Fisk gave expression to the truth that has been dumbly struggling in me for utterance. Concerning such struggles, it has been said "If you can not express yourself on any subject, struggle until you can. ... Struggle to re-express some truth of God to yourself, and God will use that expression to someone else.[2]" .... "Study to shew thyself approved unto God, a workman that needeth not to be ashamed, rightly dividing the word of truth." (2Tim 2:15)

May my struggles find the expression in this short booklet which will clarify a gross error in soteriology that has plagued Christians since its inception in the mind of St. Augustine (AD 354-430). That error is in considering some chosen and elected for salvation, and some chosen and elected for damnation. The doctrine of election has even been that distorted in some Regular Baptist Churches that I have attended. This booklet is dedicated to the hope that it will keep some from partaking in the crippling poison of that error and give expression to a truth that has been struggling in you for utterance.

This effort was prompted by the airing of Dr. R.C. Sproul's series called "Predestination." The error broadcast in that airing inflamed righteous indignation and sent me on a quest to express the truth concerning the Biblical doctrine of election. Thank you Dr. R.C. Sproul! Your error has initiated the struggle and it has been for my betterment.

---

[1]   Chambers, Oswald, "*My Utmost For His Highest*"

Table of Contents

A Word About the Author

Pastor Rice is a retired USAF Systems Engineer with a Masters of Science degree and 48 years of being a born-again Baptist by conviction. He has been a youth worker and associate pastor for 20 years of his military career and has been a senior pastor since his retirement in 1995. His upbringing and work in Regular Baptist Churches, his associate pastorate in a Southern Baptist Church and his staunch stand as an Independent Baptist Pastor have given him a broad background for teaching Biblical Doctrine. His 36 hours of graduate level Bible Seminary work and weekly communication of doctrine combine with his systems analyst background to enliven a fresh look at Biblical Doctrines and Systematic Theology. Pastor Rice's staunch stand on the inerrant, infallible, verbally inspired Word of God make all his works Biblically accurate and adherent to the Holy Scriptures. His fervent love for the Saviour and Redeemer of mankind resonates in his writings on Bible doctrine.

Chapter 1 Introduction – The Dilemma

The dangerous tentacles of Reformed Augustinian doctrine have invaded our theology to squeeze out Biblical truth and literal Biblical interpretation. We need to learn to recognize the syntax of these tentacles and speak out against the errors which are especially menacing when it comes to a sound doctrine of election and predestination. Believe the Bible or believe Reformed Augustinian doctrine. You can not do both.

Isaiah 53:6 says "All we like sheep have gone astray; we have turned every one to his own way; and the LORD hath laid on him the iniquity of us all." The late noted Evangelist Loren Dawson said:

> "This verse begins and ends with 'all.' If the first 'all' is without exception, and it is, what gives us the right, what hermeneutic or homiletic gives us the right to say that the last all is just for a few selected ones? That kind of shoots limited atonement in the foot doesn't it. ... God doesn't make that choice, you make that choice! The only thing in this world that is needed to bring down that idol of TULIP Theology is knowing that God in sovereign grace gives man a choice and then holds men accountable to that choice! That just shoots their idol in the head and it all comes down just like Nebuchadnezzar's idol of gold and the wind blows it all away."

The gross error found in 5 point Calvinism permeates our theology with a poison. That poison has paralyzed soul winning, hushed prayer closets and stifled our knowledge of God and His will. Their TULIP idol of gold has already been declared dead. Paul Freeman shows us its epitaph:

> "Concerning the Five Points of Calvinism, in *The Reformed Doctrine of Predestination,* Lorain Boettner has stated, 'prove any one of them true and all of the others will follow as logical and necessary parts of the system. Prove any one of them false and the whole system must be abandoned!' Mr. Boettner is considered an authority on the subject, so I would encourage you to follow his advice. Abandon the system when you find any one of the Five Points to be wrong.[2]"

The idol has been brought down and this work is intended to make the dangerous pieces turn into 'the chaff of the summer threshing floor' (Dan 2:35) and God can stir the wind that carries those pieces away, 'that no place can be found for them'.

---

[2] Freeman, Paul L., *"What's Wrong With Five Point Calvinism"*

Many works have been published which dispel the errant TULIP model espoused by Calvinism. Many works are available which dispel the errant on-again-off-again will-full salvation of Arminianism. This examination exposes the deep roots of both errors and is intended to lead you into a sound Biblical stance on a sound Biblical doctrine of election and predestination. The sovereignty of God and mans free-will will be examined and balanced. God's foreknowledge will be coupled with the understanding that God only foreordained certain events, not all events.

Some who have been trained to hold onto some footholds of Calvinism lest they be swept into an Arminian camp will find this search disturbing. Theological speech has been slurred toward Augustinian error and this work will expose that speech impediment. Some who have been trained to discard Calvin but hold on to a foreknowledge solution for election will find this search disturbing. These clearly state that God does not predestine one's election to heaven or to hell but then they say "He just 'foreknows' who will be saved and who will be lost." Again St. Augustine of Hippo, North Africa, has slurred their thinking so badly that they cannot properly pronounce "Free Will." Such a 'foreknowledge' view makes it difficult to speak plainly about how "prayer changes things." Some may find this search disturbing or unsettling but all should find it thought provoking and rewarding.

What you believe controls what you do. When you believe (albeit behind the scenes of conscience thought) that salvation is already determined in God's foreknowledge, fervent prayers that could change the eternal destiny of souls will not be found in your prayer closet. Whether you get disturbed in this quest or not, please explore with me the deep seated errors of Reformed Augustinian doctrine as touching election and predestination, sovereignty and foreknowledge. Exploring these roots of error has brought about various and sometimes hostile reactions by my Baptist brethren. I trust yours will be one which says "Search me, O God, and know my heart: try me, and know my thoughts: And see if *there be any* wicked way in me, and lead me in the way everlasting." (Psalm 139:23-24) I pray that it does.

Before examining the Biblical doctrine of election and predestination we need to go back into history and find out where the erroneous views originated and how they developed. It is rightly called reformed Augustinian doctrine. Bishop Augustine of Hippo cultured it and the protestant reformers extracted it from Roman Catholicism. They then developed it into an ill fated TULIP. It has been called Calvinism because John Calvin riddled it throughout the Geneva Bible. It has been defended by the prince of Baptist Preachers in his work "A Defense of Calvinism" by Charles Haddon Spurgeon. Spurgeon surely did believe in eternal security, and did not want to be called Arminian. The complete history of the false doctrine of election is worthy of some of our study time.

Chapter 2 **Origins of the Error**

Baptists distinctively use only the Holy Scripture to determine all of their faith and practice. Various ideas, doctrines and theologies departing from the clear teaching of Scripture are ever present and attract large followings down broad ways. Augustinian theology coagulated into John Calvin's errors which solidified in the reformed thinking called Calvinism. At its heart it removes the free will decision from the salvation experience. It has been stated by the historian Herbert S. Skeats, that:

> "It is the singular and distinguished honor of the Baptists to have repudiated from their earliest history all coercive power over the consciences and actions of men with reference to religion. They were the proto-evangelists of the voluntary principle."[3]

One of the best tools to continue this repudiation, is to expose the origins of the errors around election and predestination and examine how these origins depart from Holy Scripture. Then seeing the growth and development of this error into a full fledged false doctrine is both alarming and enlightening at the same time.

The grossest errors of Saint Augustine center around an over riding authority of 'The Church' and, center stage in this consideration is a 'compulsory salvation'. Augustine twisted and hyper extended Scripture unmercifully to arrive at, and defend these doctrines. The ugly twists still permeate the theology books of our day. The tentacles of error underlie the misunderstandings and misrepresentations of Calvinism and Arminianism for every Christian who would study "So Great Salvation"[4] from the Bible. Briefly examine now these origins of error.

---

[3] Skeats, Herbert S., English historian (1688-1891), *"History of the Free Churches of England"*, (Unknown Binding - 1891)

[4] Heb 2:2-4 "For if the word spoken by angels was stedfast, and every transgression and disobedience received a just recompence of reward; How shall we escape, if we neglect **so great salvation**; which at the first began to be spoken by the Lord, and was confirmed unto us by them that heard *him*; God also bearing *them* witness, both with signs and wonders, and with divers miracles, and gifts of the Holy Ghost, according to his own will?"

Augustinian Error

Augustinian error fell from St. Augustine (AD 354 - 480) Bishop of Hippo, North Africa, in two major areas. The first in the doctrine of the church, the second in the doctrine of salvation. The two areas of error met where salvation was compulsory. In Augustin's mind salvation could be forced upon a soul by infant baptism or by his doctrine of the two swords, wielded by the Roman Church. But he also devised that God himself had to force salvation on to totally depraved souls by His sovereignty. All the errors of catholicism are in embryo stage in the teachings of Augustine.[5] So too, is the predestination errors of Calvinism.

These errors came to full and wretched bloom in the Roman Catholic Imperial Church of the medieval period. When Constantine (AD 306-337) saw the political advantage of replacing the mandatory Roman paganism with a mandatory 'Christian' paganism he locked arms with the Roman Church and brought a second sword, a steel sword, into their mix. The Church at Rome took the allegorizing of Augustine and concluded with him that Jesus said to sell your garments and buy swords and that two swords are sufficient[6] (Luke 22:38)

Constantine commanded that there be 'one state ordered religion' for 'one unified empire.' This scheme used God's Sword of the Spirit, supposedly wielded by the Roman Church, united with Man's Sword of Steel wielded by a magistrate to force the Kingdom of God upon all the unified Roman Empire. What became called Constantinianism, (or compulsory Christianity, vs. voluntary salvation by faith via free will) is found in its embryonic stage in Augustin's theology. Leonard Verduin writes in *"The Reformers and Their Stepchildren"* [7]

---

5   Anderson, Sir Robert, *"The Bible Or The Church"*, 2nd ed., London: Pickering and Inglis, n.d., quoted "The Roman Church was molded by Augustine into the form it has ever since maintained. Of all the errors that later centuries developed in her teaching, there is scarcely one that cannot be found in embryo in his writings."

6   St. Augustine of Hippo, *"The Writings Against The Manichaeans And Against The Donatists"* LC Call no:BR60, Palm copy pp338, html npnf104 iv.ix.XIX page_195

7   Verduin, Leonard, *"The Reformers And Their Stepchildren"* Grand Rapids Wm. B. Eerdmans Pub. Co. @1964 p 65

"It was Augustine, he perhaps more than any other, who supplied the Constantinians with arguments from the Scriptures (or rather with arguments fastened upon the Scriptures) whereby coercion was rendered theologically respectable. The expression found in Luke 14:23, "*Constrain them to come in*," rendered in Latin *Compelle intrare,* was exactly what he needed in his running battle with the Donatists.

"The followers of Donatus were offering to secede from the "fallen" Church and to go their own way, a step which the advocates of "Christian sacralism" (Constantinianism) could not permit, for it would strike at the very heart of their dream of a faith common to all in the empire. Hence they let it be known, early in the conflict, that schism would not be permitted but would be opposed, if need be with arms. Thereupon the Donatists pointed out that this would be to deviate from the policies of the Master, who had not raised a finger, much less a sword, to restrain people from going away. More than that, when a sizable group walked out He had confronted His disciples with the wistful question, "Do you not also want to go?[8]"

"To this line of thought – the cogency of which had not escaped him – Augustine replied:

"I hear that you are quoting that which is recorded in the Gospel, that when the seventy followers went back from the Lord they were left to their own choice in this wicked and impious desertion and that He said to the twelve remaining 'Do you not also want to go?' But what you fail to say is that at the time the Church was only just beginning to burst forth from the newly planted seed and that the saying had not yet been fulfilled in her "All kings shall fall down before Him, all nations shall serve him." It is in proportion to the more enlarged fulfillment of this prophecy that the Church now wields greater power – so that she may now not only invite but also compel men to embrace that which is good." (Augustine's *Letter to Donatus,* No. 173 as printed in *Select Library of Nicene and Post Nicene Fathers,* ed, Philip Schaff, Vol. 1.)

"Here we have an early representation of the notion that the Church of Christ was intended by its Founder to enter into a situation radically different from the one depicted in the New Testament. Here we have the beginnings of the notion , which reigned supreme in the minds of men all through the medieval times, that part way into the Christian era a change was intended by the King of the Church himself – a change whereby the world of apostolic times would become obsolete. This change was identified with the Constantinian innovation. This idea set forth by Augustine controlled the thought and the theology of European man all through medieval times. It led to all sorts of theological absurdities ... "

The theological absurdity that God preselected individual souls

---

[8] It should not surprise anyone but should here be noted that Augustine of Hippo, AD 345-480, did not quote the 1611 King James English of John 6:67"Will ye also go away?" Augustine was more into Latin.

for salvation and forces his will on them with an irresistible grace is but one of the problems of Augustinian's compulsory salvation theology. His compulsory salvation via infant baptism, via 'be baptized' or 'be burned' or via God's sovereignty has caused many a Baptist, Anabaptist, Donatist, Waldensian, and Believer their martyrdom. Baptists needn't lean toward it in any form today, especially not in the realm of election or foreordained salvation of some individuals.

Augustine gets worse in his error as he continues to allegorize and misconstrue Scripture as follows:

> "This (namely the 'enlarged fulfillment' idea which now puts the Church in position to coerce) He (Christ) shows plainly enough in the parable of the wedding feast; after He had summoned the invited ones ... and the servants have said 'It has been done as you ordered and yet there is room' the Master said 'Go out in the highways and hedges and compel them to come in in order that my house may be full.' Now observe how that it was 'bring them in' and not 'compel them,' by which the incipient condition of the Church is signified, during which she was but growing toward the position of being able to compel. Since it was right by reason of greater strength and power to coerce men to the feast of eternal salvation therefore it was said later ... 'Go out into the highways and hedges and compel them to come in.' " (Augustine's *Letter to Donatus,* No. 173)

He goes on with his theology of coercion into the kingdom with this taunt to Donatists:

> "And so if you (Donatists) were strolling quietly outside the feast of eternal salvation and the unity of the holy Church then we would overtake you on your 'highways'; but now that you verily by many injuries and cruelties which you perpetrate upon our people, are full of thorns and spines, now we come upon you in your 'hedges' to compel you. The sheep which is compelled is coerced while it is unwilling, but after it has been brought in it may graze as its own volition wills. (Augustine's *Letter to Donatus,* No. 173)

Leonard Verduin, researching for the "Calvin Foundation" itself, shows in his book these Scripture twisting, aberrant theology forming quotes of Augustine. He also demonstrates his antecedent role in Constantinianism, or compulsory salvation by a sword wielding, infant baptizing Church. We, here, understand them as forming another large theological blunder concerning compulsory salvation in the doctrine of predestination that would bloom into its ugly TULIP under John Calvin. Again, we reiterate in the Biblical doctrine of election that salvation is always a free will voluntary decision of a free moral agent. It is never compulsory. It is never to be coerced, not by a Roman sword, not by the baptism of an infant, not by a decree of God, not by a doctrine of election , not by a foreordaining of individuals to salvation, and not by a fatalistic foreknowledge of God. Not coerced, nor mandated in any way by man nor God, it is ever left as the voluntaryanism of *"Whosoever will may come."*

The Vulgar Vulgate Errors

The Latin Vulgate Bible was translated by Jerome between 382 and 405 AD. This translation, a contemporary of St Augustine's fallacies (Agustine 354 - 480 AD) contained many translation errors which seeded misinterpretations in both Catholicism and then, in turn in Reformer's Calvinism. The three 'P's that should immediately come to mind with the Vulgar Vulgate are priests, penance and predestination. Priest craft, came from the mistranslation of 'presbytery'; paying penance, came from the mistranslation of Biblical 'repentance'; and predestination of souls, came from the overpowering mistranslation of the Greek 'proorizo'. This word does not mean predestine! its meaning is 'to decide beforehand', with no connection with God's decreeing, predestining, or deciding before creation.

These three Vulgate mistranslations were not accidental. Jerome was pandering to the errant theology of his day when he included the avenues for priest craft, man paid penance, and a God decreed destiny of souls and life events. This is a powerful allegation. We should include some of the supporting references. In his *"General Introduction to the study of the Holy Scripture"* F.E. Gigots, a leading catholic authority states:

> "The Vulgate can be charged, indeed, with innumerable faults, inaccuracies, inconsistencies and arbitrary dealing in particulars... the high place the Vulgate holds even to this day in the Roman Church, where it is unwarrantably and perniciously placed on an equality with the original."[9]

Samuel Berger goes on to point out more specific errors in *"Cambridge History of the Bible"* stating:

> "We might also point out certain number of passages in which the

---

[9] Gigots, F.E.,*"General Introduction to the study of the Holy Scripture"* p324-5)

translation assumes a dogmatic or moral bearing which seems to be outside that of the original. Those are serious defects in our translation of the Holy Writ. ...Well known examples of 'far reaching errors' include the whole system of Catholic 'penance', drawn from the Vulgate's "do penance" ... when the Latin should, of course, have followed the Greek "repent." Likewise the word "sacrament" was a mis-rendering from the Vulgate of the original word "mystery." Even more significant, perhaps, was the rendering of the word "presbyter" (elder) as 'priest!' ...

"Thus the Vulgate became the most vulgarized and bastardized text imaginable. ...

"This Vulgate was taken to England and became the basis of the Christianity with such deep root in that rich soil ... error and all."[10]

In his book *"An Introduction to the Textual Criticism of the New Testament"*, A.T. Robertson says of Henslow's book:

"he has a striking section on 'the Vulgate as the source of false doctrines.' It is difficult to estimate the influence of the Vulgate on all modern versions..."[11]

The term 'predestination' alas comes from the Vulgate. In Acts 13:48, the Vulgate has 'praeordinati' unfairly; Augustine's English for 'destinati' is much too strong a word and the phrase '*as many as were ordained* (Latin-praeordinati, but Greek-tasso) *to eternal life believed*' is used off hand to 'prove' election of individuals. You see, Vulgate error invades Calvin's doctrine of Election.

Dean Henry Alford, student of the original Greek renders this verse (Acts 13:48) "as many as were disposed to eternal life," then adds "by whom so disposed is not here declared!"[12]

Samuel Fisk has a whole section showing this error and demonstrates in part with:

"Bishop Wadsworth himself, a gifted linguist, authority on the Vulgate and commentator on the text of the New Testament (The New Testament in the Original Greek, with Introduction and notes") states , "It would be interesting to inquire, what influence these renderings in the Vulgate version had on the minds of some, like St. Augustine and his followers in the Western Church, in treating the great questions of Free will, Election, Reprobation and Final Perseverance. What also was the result of that

10 Berger, Samuel, *"Cambridge History of the Bible"* Vol III, p 414.
11 Robertson, A.T., *"An Introduction to the Textual Criticism of the New Testament"*, p128,
12 Alford, Dean Henry, *"The New Testament for English Reading Acts"* p745

influence on the minds of some writers of the Reformed Churches who rejected the authority of Rome, which almost canonized that version (the Vulgate), and yet in these two important texts (Acts 2:47, and Acts 13:48) where swayed away by it from the sense of the originals.

"The tendency of the Eastern (Greek) Fathers who read the original Greek was in a different direction from that of the Western school; and Calvinism can receive no support from these 2 texts as they stand in the original words of inspiration, and as they were expanded by the primitive Church (from "The Acts of the Apostles" p108)

"On Acts 2:47 Cooks Commentary[13] ... and on 'were ordained' in Acts 13:48 it states ... followed the Vulgate. Rather 'were set in order for, i.e. 'disposed for eternal life'; as in the Syriac, or the passive of this verb being used as equivalent to the middle."[14]

We see from this very brief examination that translation errors in the Latin Vulgate greatly propagated the error of individual election first conceived by St. Augustine. The gross error plummeted through centuries of Roman Catholic salvation by coercion and then took root in John Calvin's fertile ground of misconceptions concerning these Scriptures.

What the Bible Says:

These two verses (Acts 2:47, and Acts 13:48) are badgered about so, it is important to see them accurately translated without a Latin, Catholic or Calvinistic influence. Of coarse we know that the King James translation has the superior text, the superior translators, the superior technique and the superior theology in its translation.[15] Thus, here they are in that superior translation:

Acts 2:47 "Praising God, and having favor with all the people. And the Lord added to the church daily such as should be saved."

Acts 13:48 "And when the Gentiles heard this, they were glad, and glorified the word of the Lord: and as many as were ordained to eternal life believed."

---

[13] Any views and hostility toward the AV expressed here by Cooks Commentary, here being quoted by Fisk, is certainly not shared by this author. Textual critics often state that even the AV 'often followed' the vulgar Vulgate within their more shallow arguments. This argument is baseless. Here the effect of the Vulgate is traced into doctrine and modernist bibles, but that trace does not denigrate the King James Authorized Version of the Holy Bible.

[14] Fisk, Samuel, "*Calvinistic Paths Retraced*" pp 69-70

[15] Waite, D.A., Th.D., Ph.D. "*The Case for the King James Bible*"

The clear emphasis in both is that only the saved, i.e. converted, born again ones, get added to the Church. There is no indication that there is a pre-ordaining towards salvation in either verse.

With great consistency, every time the Greek word 'tasso' was used in the Bible (8 times) as a perfect tense, passive voice, participle (2 of the 8 times in Acts 13:48 and Rom 13:1) it was properly translated 'ordain' by the King James translators. Ordain contains in its definition: 'to put in order'. And it is clear that those in Acts 13:48 were put in order to receive eternal life by their conversion not by any predestination. The point is, only the converted were added. We should be so careful to add only the truly converted, born again ones, to our local Church.

What of John Calvin and the Error

The election and predestination theology of John Calvin (1509 – 1564) came, not from the Bible, but because he learned to speak the Reformed Augustinian error. John Calvin popularized three prominent theological errors[16]. He supported a strong Church dominated state[17], the baptism of infants by sprinkling, and the election of souls for salvation by predestination.

A short study shows that John Calvin had nothing to do with the 5 points of Calvinism. His error, instead, had these three major points, a State's Church, an infant's baptism and a soul's predestination. He believed Augustine's teachings that man could not make the

---

[16] Stringer, Dr. Phil, *"The Faithful Baptist Witness"*, Landmark Baptist Press, 1998, p138

[17] Stringer, Ibid, p131 quoted "Often persecutors have expressed great sorrow at bing 'forced' to persecute non-conformists, and having 'no other option.' Jerome Bolsec, a physician in Geneva, Switzerland, began to challenge John Calvin's explanation of predestination and election. ... When Calvin could not convince him to change his doctrine, he and the city council of Geneva had Bolsec arrested. After a long trial, he was banished from Geneva for life. Not long after Bolsec was banished, Michael Servetus was executed in Geneva for holding 'heretical' views on the deity of Christ (he, in fact, denied the deity of Christ.) and baptism (he was opposed to infant baptism.) Calvin expressed great sorrow at both incidents. He could not (or would not) allow people to disagree with his thinking, so he had no choice but to participate in these and other persecutions. ... Calvin and Luther both put their stamp of approval upon the execution of Baptists, and Zwingli actually participated in such persecution."

decision for Salvation by any use of free will, and thus one's salvation was compulsory by God's sovereignty alone. He was in error to believe Augustine's teaching that if God predetermined those who would be saved and those who would be lost, he must have done it in an infinite plan before the foundation of the earth. And then he was in error to believe the Augustinian folly that since election of individuals for salvation is required, then EVERY act, breath, and thought of man is decreed to happen, and that such 'decreeing' was done before the foundation of the earth.

Again, John Calvin reckoned that EVERYTHING was in God's infinite and unchangeable plan and Sovereign control and that this infinite plan was established and written before the foundation of the world. We will see in this study, that there is no Scripture to support such a conjecture, only Augustinian's doctrine and language. This over bearing establishment of God's decreeing every detail of ones life is expressed in his overemphasis on God's sovereignty and directly resulting underemphasis on man's free will.

The five points of Calvinism are found nowhere in Calvin's writings, but these three fallacious, un-Biblical notions are found throughout his commentaries, and tainted all his theology. Some review of his work will show that John Calvin was speaking Reformed Augustinian, not Biblical Exegesis, when he wrote his commentaries and formed his theology.

The Reformed Systemization of the TULIP Error

The 5 point hypothesized TULIP model of Calvinism came, not from the Bible, nor from John Calvin, but from a Presbyterian 'knee-jerk' reaction to James Harmensen's (1560-1609) five contentions to Augustinian errors about election and predestination. Harmensen, (in Latin Arminius, thus the name Arminianism) refused to speak Reformed Augustinian with such vehemence that his name rings clear to this day. The ring is the opposite in extreme of the 5 points called TULIP. Some have errantly been taking their corners in a 'boxing ring' on either the side of Calvinism or Arminianism ever since. Neither corner is Biblical. Some try to pick a center point in this boxing ring and call it Biblicist. One actually needs a model that would add a third dimension to our geometry and get us off this boxing ring approach. Such a dimension will be introduce in this treaties.

Robert Lewis Dabney (1820 – 1898), a noted American

Presbyterian pastor, theologian and one of Southern Presbyterianism's most influential scholars, writes on this point:

> "HISTORICALLY, this title (The Five Points of Calvinism, TULIP) is of little accuracy or worth; I use it to denote certain points of doctrine, because custom has made it familiar. Early in the seventeenth century the Presbyterian Church of Holland, whose doctrinal confession is the same in substance with ours, was much troubled by a species of new-school minority, headed by one of its preachers and professors, James Harmensen... Church and state have always been united in Holland; hence the civil government took up the quarrel. Professor Harmensen (Arminius) and his party were required to appear before the States General (what we would call Federal Congress) and say what their objections were against the doctrines of their own church, which they had freely promised in their ordination vows to teach. Arminius handed in a writing in which he named five points of doctrine concerning which he and his friends either differed or doubted. These points were virtually: Original sin, unconditional predestination, invincible grace in conversion, particular redemption, and perseverance of saints. I may add, the result was: that the Federal legislature ordered the holding of a general council of all the Presbyterian churches then in the world, to discuss anew and settle these five doctrines. This was the famous Synod of Dort, or Dordrecht, where not only Holland ministers, but delegates from the French, German, Swiss, and British churches met in 1618." [18]

The Presbyterian position has been solid since their Synod. But for Bible believers of other stripes the Reformed Augustinian errors embraced by the Presbyterians have often crept in unawares. Baptists, (once referred to as "People of the Book") who are pressured to lean to one corner or the other of this Calvinist vs Arminian boxing match, have toppled into a Calvinist pit of error and are unwittingly slurring their speech with Augustinian errors. Most Baptists now will not step as far away from Augustine's 'Doctrine of Decrees' as the Bible requires. This thesis proposes to help recognize, and correct the leanings toward this Reformed Augustinian position.

What of C. H. Spurgeon's Defense of Calvinism?

A Presbyterian Clergy that responded to a letter to R.C. Sproul's organization curtly commented that "small minds should let Spurgeon be their spokesman when it comes to wording a Baptist position about Calvinism." Charles Haddon Spurgeon (1834-1892), the 'Prince of Preachers' was indeed a British Reformed Baptist

---

[18]   R.L. Dabney *"The Five Points of Calvinism"*

Preacher. He did indeed write "*A Defense of Calvinism*" which makes him highly influential amongst reformed Christians of different denominations, especially the Presbyterians. But Baptists who read his work do not relish him as their spokesman concerning the error's of Calvinism. He spoke a noticeable twang of Reformed Augustinian in this defense, but more so, he articulated a staunch position against the fluctuations and doctrinal irresponsibleness of Arminianism. Baptists do hold to his brazen denial of Arminian's doctrinal error, but not to his leanings toward Augustinian theology. Spurgeon states that:

> "The old truth that Calvin preached, that Augustine preached, that Paul preached, is the truth that I must preach to-day, or else be false to my conscience and my God. I cannot shape the truth; I know of no such thing as paring off the rough edges of a doctrine. John Knox's gospel is my gospel. That which thundered through Scotland must thunder through England again."—C. H. Spurgeon

Indeed, Spurgeon became a well cited spokesman for the errant doctrine of Calvinism's Predestination. This entanglement with error is a result of excessive esteem for the Catholic's Saint Augustine, and the Protestant's John Calvin. As he states it:

> "You may take a step from Paul to Augustine, then from Augustine to Calvin, and then-well, you may keep your foot up a good while before you find such another." When he visited the Simplon Hospice, he said, "I was delighted to find that they are Augustine monks, because, next to Calvin, I love Augustine. I feel that Augustine was the great mine out of which Calvin digged his mental wealth; and the Augustine monks, in practicing their holy charity, seemed to say: 'Our Master was a teacher of grace, and we will practice it, and give without money and without price to all comers whatsoever they need.[19]

Spurgeon's leaning into error is well illustrated in his conversation with a peer:

> "When Mr. Spurgeon went, years ago, to preach for Dr. Clifford, whose church was then at Praed Street, he said in the vestry before the service, "I cannot imagine, Clifford, why you do not come to my way of thinking," referring to his Calvinistic views.
> "Well," answered John Clifford, "you see, Mr. Spurgeon, I only see you

---

[19] Fullerton, William Young, "*Charles Haddon Spurgeon A Biography*", Chapter 20 pg 184 (soft copy), Spurgeon Archive, www.spurgeon.org, Internet Book, accessed Aug 2007

about once a month, but I read my Bible every day."[20]

For his defense of Calvinism, Protestants continually cite Spurgeon as a Baptist spokesman, and Baptists lean on his authority to travel on this garden path of predestinational error. This is the unfortunate side of C. H. Spurgeon's otherwise immaculate legacy. His tomb reads:

Here lies the body of
Charles Haddon Spurgeon
waiting for the appearing of his
Lord and Saviour Jesus Christ.

On the other side of the tomb is the verse of the hymn he was accustomed to write in albums:

E'er since by faith I saw the stream
Thy flowing wounds supply,
Redeeming love has been my theme,
And shall be till I die.[21]

Even though Spurgeon dragged Augustin's error into Baptist circles, his theme was always the redeeming love of Christ available to whosoever would believe. In his preaching it was profoundly clear that your fate for all eternity depended on what you personally did with the Only Begotten Son of God, and not on what God may have decided before the foundation of the world.

C.H. Spurgeon's work *"A Defense of Calvinism "*[22] would be better titled "A Defense of the Gospel." Although he mentions in passing three points of the Calvinist TULIP, he does not articulate an acceptance of their model as much as he rejects the Arminian model, there being only these two choices in popular view in the 1800s.
Conventionally there has been a straight line between Calvinism and Arminianism and you must plot out a position on that line. In this treaties we will establish a triangle model rather than a straight line model.

---

[20]   ibid Chapter 13 pg 135 (soft copy)
[21]   ibid Chapter 20 pg 188 (soft copy)
[22]   Spurgeon, Charles Haddon, *"A Defense of Calvinism"*
       http://www.spurgeon.org/calvinis.htm

Spurgeon stayed on the line positioned toward the Calvinist's half. You and I can step off the line and become Biblicists. To understand better where a Biblicist would differ from Spurgeon's defense let's look at a condensed outline of his "*Defense of Calvinis*m."

On pages 1-15[23], Spurgeon defends the steadfast everlasting nature of one's salvation against the shallow fickleness of the Arminian model. Baptists hold dogmatically to this eternal security position.

On pages 15-30 he develops that salvation is all of grace and none of works. Again, the Bible and Baptists are clear on this point and likewise contend with the fickle Arminian model on this point.

On pages 30-60 he develops an "epitome of Calvinism" which he contends to be "Salvation is of the Lord." His continual emphasis throughout, as is ours, is that salvation is by grace and not by works. In this section he uses 5 pages to purport that God loved him, and chose him before the foundation of the world. He uses no Scripture, for such a declaration, only a mocking slander against an Arminian preacher. Spurgeon therein regurgitates the baseless Augustinian doctrine that election of individual souls took place before the foundation of the world, but he does know better than try to find a Biblical defense of such tripe, there is none. Again he is more so rejecting Arminianism than defending Calvinism.

In pages 60-90 Spurgeon graciously speaks for John Wesley and his doctrine of whosoever will. He points out the dilemma between his own belief in election and the Wesley Brother's Biblical position on the free will of man. He defends his holding to the idea of decrees in this dilemma, but graciously backs away from a hard line Calvinistic model. Based on his own salvation experience, Spurgeon concludes that God must have chosen him, because he would never have chosen God. God must have orchestrated each event in his life, because they alone brought him to God. In this study we will learn that God's calling and wooing does not make for God's choosing and electing. In this study we will delineate that God's orchestrating of events in our lives does not necessitate a decree written before the foundation of the earth. These are things that Spurgeon wrestled with in this defense, but he never came to a clear Biblical position on election and decrees. You and I can do so more particularly.

In pages 90-100 he contends against universalism's model that

---

[23] The page numbers here are from a soft copy formatted in a pdb formatt, if you had the 12 page printout of the defense you would divide these pdb numbers by 10 to find the described information.

says, 'all of mankind is saved by Christ's sacrifice'. Baptists contend against this as well, and need to more contend with the American Bible Society and the United Bible Society which are both so aligned with this abominable universalist doctrine.

In pages 100-120 Spurgeon acknowledges that his doctrine of election completely obliterates God's doctrine of "whosoever will may come." He mentions the matter of leaning toward the "less licentious" of the two doctrines. He again speaks out against Arminianism. Then C.H. Spurgeon expertly likens the two considerations as two parallel railroad tracks that run through the Bible but do not visibly touch; but when you look way off toward the throne of God they seem to merge, but only there. Spurgeon was no Calvinist, he just believed the Bible account of so great salvation.

Baptists, however, shall not let Spurgeon be their spokesman concerning the Doctrine of Election and Predestination. He developed no Biblical basis for a pre-world election of souls, though he apparently believed it, rather than believing in an Arminian model. He developed no Biblical basis for the decrees of God to include his every thought and finger movement, though for himself, he would rather believe that, than to believe he moved toward God of his own free will. He developed no Biblical basis that God draws men with an irresistible grace, though he would rather believe that, than the Arminian preachers he heard. Spurgeon did not delineate the unBiblical errors of Reformed Augustinian doctrine of election and predestination. He reluctantly learned to speak them as his own beliefs. He could not foundation them in Scripture, though they are prevalent in theology books. You and I want to be more careful to let the Bible determine our doctrine of election and predestination.

Spurgeon and Calvin, Knox and Edwards were all great preachers, but they had their speech tainted with Reformed Augustinian. This author does not mind that they did. Nor mind that some might, but wants to educate about the slur in speech that comes from such tainted doctrine. It could be one would prefer to speak more legibly on the subject of election and predestination. It could be they will recognize Reformed Augustinian and thereby better comprehend the King's English when considering His "so great salvation."

Chapter 3 **What is Election**

To see what Biblical election is all about, lets first carefully examine the use of the term throughout the Bible. To often one goes about this examination backward. They determine what they believe about a subject, then go to the Bible trying to support their belief. For most, this is the danger involved in examining the Biblical doctrine of election and predestination. There is present an a-priori unction that election has to do with a soul receiving salvation or rejecting it. It is a bold statement but it needs to be said here: 'Nowhere in the Bible is election concerned with the eternal, heaven or hell destiny of a soul.' Always election is to *service* not to destiny. Now with any a priori belief system well shaken and on the table for examination let us begin by examining the election of Israel.

Israel was elect, a chosen nation, a chosen people. They were elect to do three major deeds;

    - to deliver the Messiah to humanity;

    - to deliver the written precepts of God to mankind; and

    - to show monotheism to the whole world.

First, through Israel we trace the chosen seed. This righteous seed goes through individuals, tribes, kings, harlots and Moabites. For seed purposes, the Bible says that Jacob was loved and Esau was hated. (Mal 1:2-3, Rom 9:13) Esau was not chosen for eternal damnation to hell in this hatred, he was just not chosen as the seed line of the Lord Jesus Christ. The seed traced from Abraham through Judah, (Gen 12:7, Gen 49:10) through David (2Sam 7:16) then for Joseph through Solomon, but for Mary through Nathan.[24] This elect seed is carefully traced to the Messiah who was to be of the tribe of Judah and the seed of David. This tracing of the seed line is a major drama of the Old Testament narrative, a drama that pits Satan against Jehovah God for the delivery of the seed that is to dash his head. (Genesis 3)

---

[24] Matthew 1 gives Joseph's lineage through Solomon while the lineage of Mary through Nathan is given in Luke 3, right after God announces of Jesus "Thou art my beloved Son." The next verse in Luke 3 designates Joseph as the son-in-law of Heli, and follows the lineage of Mary, the mother of Jesus all the way back to Adam, calling him, Adam, the other son of God in complete accord with Romans 5, and 1Cor 15's 1st Adam vs God's 'last Adam'. Awesome.

Secondly, Israel was elect to deliver the written precepts of God to mankind. (Rom 3:1-2) Through Israel the 39 books of the Bible's Old Testament were written and preserved, and through them the 27 books of the Bible's New Testament were written[25].

Thirdly, Israel was elect to show to the whole world that "the LORD our God *is* one LORD" (Deut. 6:4, Mar 12:29) and that the world's polytheism was idolatry. In Mark 12:29 Jesus called this the first of all the commandments, and through Israel this message of monotheism was manifest to the world. He says to Isaiah "Ye[26] *are* my witnesses, saith the LORD, and my servant whom I have chosen: that ye may know and believe me, and understand that I *am* he: before me there was no God formed, neither shall there be after me. I, *even* I, *am* the LORD; and beside me *there is* no saviour. I have declared, and have saved, and I have shewed, when *there was* no strange *god* among you: therefore ye *are* my witnesses, saith the LORD, that I *am* God." (Isa 43:10-12)

The election of individuals and of people in the Old Testament was thus an election to accomplish a task. Nowhere in this election of a people to do these tasks is an individual soul elected or predestined to an eternity in heaven or an eternity in hell. Election in the Old Testament is always for service, to work the purposes of God in this life, here on this earth.

As in the Old Testament where individuals are chosen to accomplish three major tasks on this earth, so in the New Testament God has chosen individuals to accomplish three major tasks on this earth. Those with this tasking are called the elect. They are not chosen because of merit, not chosen at birth, nor before creation, but they become chosen, or elect, when they are born again into the body of the Elect One, the Lord Jesus Christ. Those who are 'in Christ' are as

---

[25]   Although some have hypothesized that Luke's Greek background indicates he was not Jewish by birth. They speculate that he was thus a Gentile and a non-apostle who authored two New Testament books, the Gospel According to Luke and The Acts of the Apostles. Since tradition says he was a Jew of Antioch and a Jew of the dispersion and, in any event, Luke wrote under the auspiciousness of the Apostle Paul, a Jew of Jews, in this work we shall leave such wild hypothesizing to the skeptics.

[26]   Note here that "Ye" is plural, God is not just talking to Isaiah, but to all of Israel about her calling. In the King James English any 2nd person pronoun starting with 'Y' is plural, like ye or you-all, any starting with 'T', like thee and thou, is singular. The nominative tense (subject) is thou, the dative tense (object) is thee, just like your mother taught you not to say "Me want to play" because of the first person singular nominative is properly 'I.' This clarity is lost in all modernist Bibles.

elect as the Christ. They were not chosen to be 'in Christ' but once they are 'in Christ,' through their new birth, they are elect for three major tasks. They are elect in Him:

- to be his witnesses to the lost dying world,
- to manifest Christ in this world, and
- to be the temple the Holy Spirit of God.

Acts 1:8 says: "But ye shall receive power, after that the Holy Ghost is come upon you: and ye shall be witnesses unto me both in Jerusalem, and in all Judea, and in Samaria, and unto the uttermost part of the earth." Christians are the elect in this world to be His witnesses. The become elect when they receive the Holy Spirit. They receive the Holy Spirit when they are born-again, converted, regenerated, saved, and ... not until. Through the Church we are commissioned to preach the gospel to every creature. (Mar 16:15) We, as born again believers are to witness to every creature, even house to house, and to every nation, how God saved us, and can save anybody. They went house to house in Acts 2:46. Paul did so in Acts 20:20. We, who are in Christ, are elect to be His witnesses.

Christians are also elect in Him to be the manifestation of Christ to the lost dying world. That is why they were first called Christians; because they looked like, acted like, reacted like, and talked like the Christ. Believers are elect to be the manifestation of Christ in this world. Jesus said it this way; "Ye are the light of the world. A city that is set on an hill cannot be hid. Neither do men light a candle, and put it under a bushel, but on a candlestick; and it giveth light unto all that are in the house. Let your light so shine before men, that they may see your good works, and glorify your Father which is in heaven" (Matt 5:14-16) The apostles regularly exhort us as the elect. Peter writes to 'strangers scattered about ... elect according to the foreknowledge of God' and then tells these elect "Dearly beloved, I beseech *you* as strangers and pilgrims, abstain from fleshly lusts, which war against the soul; Having your conversation honest among the Gentiles: that, whereas they speak against you as evildoers, they may by *your* good works, which they ... " (1Pet 2:11-12) Peter is not here writing to someone who is elect for a salvation experience down the road! No, he is exhorting those who are elect for service. The Apostle Paul regularly exhorts believers to behave like elect ones, and regularly reminds believers that they are the elect, because they are 'in Christ' not as if they will get 'in Christ.' Note his wording in Col 3:12-13, "Put on therefore, as the elect of God, holy and beloved, bowels of mercies, kindness, humbleness of mind, meekness,

19

longsuffering; Forbearing one another, and forgiving one another, if any man have a quarrel against any: even as Christ forgave you, so also *do ye*." This is not a challenge to those who are elect for salvation. It is a charge that the elect in Christ might be the manifestation of Christ in this world. A charge to the elect to the service that they are chosen for now that they are 'in Christ.'

Thirdly we are elect in Him as a people to be the temple of the Holy Spirit of God in this world. The Spirit that reproves the world of sin, of righteousness and of judgment dwells only in the elect.[27] It does not dwell in one prior to salvation and no one prior to salvation can hold the title of 'elect.'The spirit enters in at salvation, one is then added to the kingdom of God, (John 3) added to the family[28] of God (as adopted, as dear children, as having a new Father) and therein we become the elect, the tabernacle of God. The late Evangelist Loren Dawson said it most clearly this way "In the Old Testament God builds a tabernacle for His people, in the New Testament God builds a people for His tabernacle." If you are saved you are the elect, the temple of the Holy Ghost. If you are yet in your sins, unsaved, not yet regenerated, no matter how much Calvin and Augustine may call you elect before the foundation of the world, you cannot be elect for this service until you are ushered into the kingdom of God. There is a time when this presence of the Holy Spirit will be taken out of the world.[29]

---

[27] John 16:7-8 "Nevertheless I tell you the truth; It is expedient for you that I go away: for if I go not away, the Comforter will not come unto you; but if I depart, I will send him unto you. And when he is come, he will reprove the world of sin, and of righteousness, and of judgment:"

[28] A believer is not automatically added to the Church of God when they are saved, nor do they become part of the Bride of Christ, when they are saved; they become family of God, brothers in Christ. The idea that all believers are immediately added to a universal (catholic) church or 'invisible' (protestant rationalized fictitious) church is nowhere found in the Bible. In the Bible one is added to the church only when one believes on Christ as their Lord and Saviour, are publicly baptized by immersion, and then united into a local church membership in order to continue in the doctrine of the apostles. Nor is the Church (local, independent, autonomous) presently the Bride of Christ; it is the chaste virgin, cleansed by the Word and kept pure for the coming of the Bridegroom to take her away; she is then, on that day, and that day alone, the Bride of Christ. Note that even in our Bible based culture a bride is only a bride on the day of her wedding. Saved ones become family and enter the kingdom but they are not in the Church, until they join with a commissioned, local, Bible believing, Christ serving Church, and they are not the Bride of Christ till the Church is caught away to be that.

[29] 2Thes 2:6-8 " And now ye know what withholdeth that he might be revealed

Until that time it is the elect who are housing the Holy Spirit of God in this world. The New Testament elect are his chosen vessels for this purpose.

As before, in the Old Testament, this New Testament election is for *service* to work God's purposes in this life on this earth. Nowhere in the use of this term is an individual soul elected to an eternity in heaven or an eternity in hell. Further, nowhere in the New Testament's presentation of election, is any individual elected or chosen prior to his acceptance of Christ as Lord and Saviour.

So how has Christendom so readily departed from this Biblical representation of who the elect are?How have even Baptists succumbed to teaching that God foreknows who will be saved and who will be lost, thus sealing fates for eternity? In studying the Biblical doctrine of election we find that Augustine was wrong when he read into Scripture the predestination of individual souls into heaven. We see that John Calvin, who systematized this error into a theology and saw it permeate the Geneva Bible, did a great travesty to truth and theology. It is clear that the reformed theologian who preaches election as the predestination of individual souls into heaven or hell is so twisting the Bible doctrine of election as to make some two fold more the child of hell. So too the Baptist who believes and preaches the individual election of souls to heaven or hell is dabbling in error and false teaching which malign his very election to service as a witness to the world, as the manifestation of the love of Christ in the world, and as a temple of the Holy Spirit to reprove the world.

Nowhere in Scripture is an individual elected *to be in* Christ. But those that are in Christ are elect. Once 'in' they are the elect for special service in this world. One does not enter the kingdom of God because he was elected to enter (Eph 2:8-9 says "for by grace are ye saved" not by election), but one becomes the elect *because* he is born into the kingdom. (Eph 2:10 says "For we are his workmanship, created in Christ Jesus unto good works, which God hath before ordained that we should walk in them.") One does not get in by election (John 3:14-19), but once 'in', one is elect and tasked to service. Again examine Col 3:12 as it clarifies that election is for work not for justification; "Put on

---

in his time. For the mystery of iniquity doth already work: only he who now letteth *will let*, until he be taken out of the way. And then shall that Wicked be revealed, whom the Lord shall consume with the spirit of his mouth, and shall destroy with the brightness of his coming:"

therefore, as the elect of God, holy and beloved, bowels of mercies, kindness, humbleness of mind, meekness, longsuffering; Forbearing one another, and forgiving one another, if any man have a quarrel against any: even as Christ forgave you, so also do ye." Now that we are in the kingdom of God, '*whosoever wills*' that are installed by grace through faith, and that not of election, we are to behave as elect ones with work to do. Again, how does one get 'in'? You must make an individual decision of your will to accept Christ as your Lord and Saviour. "For whosoever shall call upon the name of the Lord shall be saved." (Rom 10:13) Once 'in' you are elected to service for your Lord, as you walk here in this life. Ergo election is to service, not to salvation.

A table of Old Testament election and New Testament election helps clarify that election is always for service and not for an eternal destiny. It also points out the parallels in the two elections.

Old Testament Elections	*New Testament Elections*
To be the seed by which the Messiah would be brought into the world. Gen 12	To be the witness to a lost dying world that the Christ has come. Acts 1:8
To Deliver the written Word of God to the world. Rom 3:1-2	To be a manifestation of The Word, the Christ, in this world John 17
To show the world that "The LORD our God is one LORD" Deut 6:4, Mar 12:9	To be the temple of the Holy Spirit of God in this world. 1Cor 6:19-20

Can I get a witness? Yes, several. In *"Subjets Of Sovereignty,"* Andrew Telford says:

> "Nowhere in the Bible is Election connected with the salvation or damnation of a human soul. ... The most important phase of Election pertains to service ... Election has to do with service. It is God's elect who serve him." [30]

In *"The Theology Of The New Testament,"* George B. Stevens states that:

> "What was the nature and the purpose of this divine election of Israel? I answer that Paul conceives of it as a historic action of God in setting apart the Jewish nation to a special mission or function in the world as the bearer of his revelation to all mankind. ... These chapters (Rom 9-11) speak of election to a historic function or mission, not of eternal destiny. ... Theology has often applied these ideas to the subject of man's final destiny. Whatever

---

[30] Telford, Andrew *"Subjects of Sovereignty"* pp. 55-56

may be the logic of such an application, it is exegetically[31] unjustifiable. ...
Paul does not teach the doctrine of predestination which Calvin taught, nor
does he teach the doctrine as held by historic Calvinism." [32]

And in *"Word Studies In The New Testament"* Marvin R.
Vincent clarifies:

> " 'Ekloge' election ... and kindred words, to 'choose', and 'chosen' or
> 'elect', are used of God's selection of men or agencies for special missions or
> attainments; but neither here (1Thes 1:4) nor elsewhere in the New
> Testament is there any warrant for the revolting doctrine that God has
> predestined a definite number of mankind to eternal life, and the rest to
> eternal destruction."[33]

In the pages that follow the Biblical doctrine of election will be
explored. It will differ greatly from Reformed theology because it will
be based on Biblical exegesis rather than on Augustinian error. It will
contend with and dis-spell the Calvinistic theology and the reformed
TULIP [34] that sprang from the fertile protestant ground of
misrepresented Scripture from a vulgar Vulgate,[35] and the erred
doctrines that came from Alexandria Egypt.

The errors of Calvinism have crept into our Churches
unawares. Directly they have quieted soul winners, halted street
preaching, bus routes, mission outreach and visitation efforts.
Indirectly the tentacles of these errors have entangled our
understanding of how an individual comes to Christ. They have given
us the idea that God foreknows who will be saved, and it is all fixed in
the future. Thus some Baptists, who are supposed to be people of the
book, have gotten the ill conceived notion that their salvation was
foreknown before the foundation of the world. Baptists have tangled
into an idea that their lives are mapped out before the world was

---

[31] Exegesis def. (from Greek) Critical explanation or analysis of a text. To interpret.
See Glossary.

[32] Stevens, George B. *"The Theology of the New Testament"* pp. 380-386

[33] Vincent, Marvin R. *"Word Studies in the New Testament "* Vol IV p. 16

[34] Total Depravity; Unconditional Election; Limited Atonement; Irresistible Grace;
Perseverance of the Saints

[35] The Latin Vulgate of 405 AD was the Catholic accepted Bible. It is filled with
translation errors, but dominated Western Christianity until the original Greek
texts were incorporated from the Eastern Byzantine Manuscripts used in the
Greek Textus Receptus and the 1611 translation of the AV known as the King
James Bible.

created. Such ill notions are from Calvin's theology book not from God's Holy Bible.

With this brief overview of Biblical election in view we will look at some theological considerations and then explore every conceivable Scripture that might address election, predestination and foreknowledge. This is important to make sure that the theological model that we tweak free of Calvinistic error remains true to Scriptures. This treaties will clarify and show that there are not two views of election, Calvin and Arminian, but three, Calvin's error, Arminian's reactive over correction, (Arminian over emphasizing free will) and the Biblical treatment of the doctrine of election and predestination. May God bless you in your studies of this latter view.

Chapter 4 Systematic Theology Considerations

A systematic theology is developed around what the Bible says about doctrines. Doctrines are built around what the Bible says about principles and concepts. There is an ever present danger of reading into the Bible what we logically believe when it is not actually present. In that way ones systematic theology effects how they read the Bible, rather than allowing the Bible to regulate their systematic theology. This has always been the case for the doctrines of election, predestination, and foreknowledge. It is important to develop a system of thinking which captures what we know about God, but it must also be considered that there will be no simple system and any system will be limited because we are finite creatures trying to grapple with an infinite God. With that warning of failure for present systematic theologies, and warning of limitation for any such system, consider some of the pitfalls and logical dilemmas of systematic theology regarding the doctrines of election, predestination and foreknowledge.

It is imperative to start with an examination of what happens when a person is born again. Calvinism not only negates the 'whosoever wills' found in the the Bible, it destroys the working model of soteriology[36]. A good working model of soteriology will merge God's foreknowledge and man's free will. There has also been an overbearing reaction on this balance called 'Open Theology' which started with some good concepts but went far deeper into a theological quagmire than is practical or advisable.

A Soteriological Model

Christianity, being made up of those who believe that Jesus was the Christ, very literally Jehovah God in the flesh, can be separated into various groups based on their consideration of the doctrine of salvation, or the doctrine of the new birth, i.e. the

---

[36]   **so·te·ri·ol·o·gy** (sō-tîr'ē-ŏl'ə-jē) *n.* The theological doctrine of salvation as effected by Jesus. [Greek *sōtērion*, deliverance (from *sōtēr*, savior, from *saos, sōs*, safe) American Heritage Dictionary, 3rd Edition, © 1994, Softkey Internaltional Inc.

understanding of what happens when one is born again. Catholic, Episcopal, Lutheran, Presbyterian, Methodist, Baptist, Brethren, even Charismatic and non-denominationals all crumble into divided sects when one considers the 'who can be saved' , the 'how one gets saved', and the 'how long one stays saved' questions. These differences find an epicenter in what happens when one is "*born again*". Thus, this makes a hingepin for clearly distinguishing between 'Christian faiths', between denominations, and even within 'Christian movements'. There are not a multiple of correct answers here.

Using our Bible to evaluate what takes place when a person is saved, and contrasting that with the teaching of a denomination, can bring into focus many of the important differences between denominations. Establishing and understanding this root difference clarifies both intra-denominational and inter-denominational squabbling and misunderstandings about the exact syntax of other doctrinal issues. Particularly here it will help clarify and falsify the Catholic doctrine of sacraments (the 'how is salvation obtained?' question), the Reformed doctrine of election (the 'who can be saved?' question) and Arminian doctrine of perseverance (the 'how long one stays saved?' question). Clarifying these questions through a look at what happens when one is born-again, will bring into focus a majority of denominational differences within Christendom. Here, it is intended to expose the error of Calvinism.

A Biblical Model of the New Birth

There are two ways of developing a systematic model that captures what Jesus called "being born again", or "being saved", or "receiving eternal life." The one to often used is to consider 1) the preponderance of Scripture, 2) the orthodox teaching of the past and 3) the logic and philosophy of human reasoning. One then develops a model, chooses supporting verses and sticks with the model, regardless. This method has been widely used and the results take on the names of their prominent developers such as Calvinism, or Arminianism. Such models will often be defended to the death, even when their developments contradict Scripture. A second, and preferred approach, is to consider the preponderance of scripture alone, develop a systematic model, then, and only then, contrast the model with the orthodox teaching of the past. This contrast provides a sanity check but more so a completeness check of the Biblical model. One would then, and only then, consider the logic and philosophy of human reasoning to comprehend the model.

We use our deductive reasoning to comprehend Scripture, but we also have a tendency to use our reasoning to twist Scripture and make it fit into our realm of world view, philosophy and reason. Thus, where this systematic model does not fit our finite comprehension, we are not to tweak the Biblically based model, but compensate our finite understanding with the knowledge that God's thoughts are not mans thoughts.

> "Let the wicked forsake his way, and the unrighteous man his thoughts: and let him return unto the LORD, and he will have mercy upon him; and to our God, for he will abundantly pardon. For my thoughts *are* not your thoughts, neither *are* your ways my ways, saith the LORD. For *as* the heavens are higher than the earth, so are my ways higher than your ways, and my thoughts than your thoughts. (Isa 55:7-9)

We need to build our salvation model faithful to the Scriptures and be careful that our poorer understandings, our human reasoning, and our philosophy do not create a misrepresentation of 'so great salvation.'

There are five aspects in the Scripture that seem to capture completely what happens to an individual when they are 'born again.' These are 1) Conversion, 2) Regeneration, 3) Justification, 4) Baptism into Christ, and 5) Indwelling of the Holy Spirit. The new birth is likened to physical birth. There is no time delayed sequence of these events, and no process that drags them out over a period of time, but 5 immediate transactions that occur when one is born-again.

The immediacy of the new-birth, with all five portions occurring at one instant in time, is vital to the comprehension of Biblical salvation, and is key to distinguishing difference between various denominational teachings. Understanding the new-birth as just that, an event in time, for an individual, where all five of these ingredients come together and take place simultaneously, clarifies, distinguishes, and safeguards the Biblical teaching from most doctrinal error and 'another gospels'.[37] The hinge pin that distinguishes most

---

[37] Paul is bold against this error in Galatians where in 1:8- 9 he says "But though we, or an angel from heaven, preach any other gospel unto you than that which we have preached unto you, let him be accursed. As we said

clearly between doctrines and denominations is how far they will separate any of these 5 events from one another and take them out of a distinct, individual, personal salvation experience. An example developed later but given here for illustration, is the timing of the occurrence of regeneration within the Reformed & Presbyterian doctrine. Many holding to a predestined individual soul election contend that a soul in sin is totally depraved, so depraved he is incapable of turning one fiber of his being towards the redeeming act of salvation. Thus before that person could start down a path that would lead to conversion, he must be regenerated. Regeneration, then is separated from the other events above, and made an event that precedes the new birth. Some would go so far as to place the regenerative act at conception or birth of an individual. This is done to fit their model and philosophy of election, even though it clearly disintegrates the Biblical model of the new birth. We can carefully develop the timing of these five and demonstrate that in Scripture they all occur simultaneously. Then we simply stick tenaciously to the Scriptures as a Biblicist would.

With this basic model of the new birth, we should define each of these 5 ingredients of the new birth. Another paper[38] shows in more depth how each systematically falls out of the Scriptures and how they are tied together in time as a single event. Briefly examine each event here.

Conversion is the turning from sin to Christ. This is the human initiation in the salvation transaction. It equally involves turning from sin and turning to Christ, you can not have one side without the other and still have this transaction complete. It involves a completeness in turning from sin and a completeness in turning to Christ in faith. God is not interested in making any new or special deals here; so one must wholly repent and turn from sin (singular) and wholly grasp Christ in faith, letting go of all else for the security of his soul. Conversion is thus repentance and faith together, as Paul so testified "how I kept back nothing that was profitable *unto you*, but have shewed you, and have taught you publicly, and from house to house,

---

before, so say I now again, If any man preach any other gospel unto you than that ye have received, let him be accursed." (Gal 1:8-9)

[38] Rice, Edward G. "*A Biblical Understanding of The New Birth Clarifies Doctrines about Sacraments, Election, and Perseverance of Saints*," published on line at GSBaptistChurch.com /seminary /soteriology/soter00.lwp/odyframe.htm

Testifying both to the Jews, and also to the Greeks, **repentance toward God, and faith toward our Lord Jesus Christ**." (Acts 20:20-21)

Regeneration is "that act of God by which new, spiritual life is implanted in man whereby the governing disposition of the soul is made holy by the Holy Spirit through truth as the means."[39] Dr. W. Vanhetloo gave here the best one sentence definition of regeneration that I have seen. It generally shows up in our Bible as 'quickening.' Jesus defines it thus "For as the Father raiseth up the dead, and quickeneth *them*; even so the Son quickeneth whom he will. For the Father judgeth no man, but hath committed all judgment unto the Son: That all *men* should honour the Son, even as they honour the Father. He that honoureth not the Son honoureth not the Father which hath sent him. Verily, verily, I say unto you, He that heareth my word, and believeth on him that sent me, hath everlasting life, and shall not come into condemnation; but is passed from death unto life. Verily, verily, I say unto you, The hour is coming, and now is, when the dead shall hear the voice of the Son of God: and they that hear shall live." (John 5:21-25) Once we were dead, then we were quickened, now we will live forever.

Justification is best defined by Scripture in 2Cor 5:21 "For he hath made him (Christ) *to be* sin for us, who knew no sin; that we might be made the righteousness of God in him." Being saved from the condemnation of sin is coming under the umbrella of what Christ did for us. Justification then is a heavenly judicial declaration of 1) remission of sin and of 2) restoration to God. This is a declarative justification, as proclaimed in Romans, not the demonstrative justification called for in the book of James[40].

Baptism into Christ often called the union with Christ, this is literally being united with Christ. Again probably best defined by Scripture in Christ's prayer in John 17:21-23 "That they all may be one; as thou, Father, *art* in me, and I in thee, that they also may be one in us: that the world may believe that thou hast sent me. 22 And the glory which thou gavest me I have given them; that they may be one, even as we are one: 23 I in them, and thou in me, that they may be made perfect in one; and that the world may know that thou hast sent me, and hast loved them, as thou hast loved me."

Indwelling of the Holy Spirit is the actual literal moving into our bodies by the Holy Spirit of God where by he now permanently

---

[39]   Dr. W. Vanhetloo's Syllabus of *Soteriology* #404 Spr 94, Page 42, Calvary Baptist Theological Seminary

[40]   There are two different definitions of justification that one must recognize before reconciling what God says through Paul and what God says through James. Both are inspired truth, that at first glance seem to clash. They do not.

indwells us. Again scripture pictures this superbly in 1Cor 6:19 "What? Know ye not that your body is the temple of the Holy Ghost *which* is in you, which ye have of God, and ye are not your own? For ye are bought with a price: therefore glorify God in your body, and in your spirit, which are God's." Also Rom 8:9 "But ye are not in the flesh, but in the Spirit, if so be that the Spirit of God dwell in you. Now if any man have not the Spirit of Christ, he is none of his." When one is saved, the Holy Spirit of God takes up residence inside them, he indwells them.

Our purpose here is not to define and develop these 5 transactions that occur at salvation, but to demonstrate that Biblically they must all occur at an instant in time, the instant one is 'born-again'. Again our emphasis is on the marvelous revelation that all five parts of this so-great-salvation are instantaneous and united transactions. Making this connection is what will allow us to clearly differentiate the various errors of 'another gospel' and thus denominational differences. We can use this understanding of conversion as the hingepin to evaluate and bring into focus all other 'Christian' doctrines and differences. This Biblical model of salvation castigates a Calvinistic doctrine of election whereby one is regenerated as a precursor to their salvation. A Calvinist will hold tenaciously to their model, even when the preponderance of Scripture disallow it.

Some Problems With Foreknowledge

Systematic theology finds challenge in melding the 'whosoever wills' in the Bible, with the 'elect according to the foreknowledge of God' in Reformed Theology. This challenge is more broadly considered in rationalizing man's free will with God's sovereignty and God's foreknowledge and God's omniscience.

In defending his belief in decrees Augustus H. Strong, solidifies a problem we face in defining foreknowledge. He states that decrees, by which God has rendered certain all the events of the universe, past, present, and future, can be proven from finite reasoning about divine foreknowledge. Stating that:

> "Foreknowledge implies fixity, and fixity implies decree. From eternity God foresaw all the events of the universe as fixed and certain. This fixity and certainty could not have had its ground either in blind fate or in the variable wills of men, since neither of these had an existence. It could have had its ground in nothing outside the divine mind, for in eternity nothing existed beside the divine mind. But for this fixity there must have been a

30

cause; if anything in the future was fixed, something must have fixed it. This fixity could have had its ground only in the plan and purpose of God. In fine, if God foresaw the future as certain, it must have been because there was something in himself which made it certain; or in other words, because He had decreed it, ... while decree does not chronologically precede, it does logically proceed foreknowledge. Foreknowledge is not of possible events, but of what is certain to be. ... An event must be made certain, before it can be known as a certain event."[41]

For the reformed theologian foreknowledge requires and implies that every breath, every hair and every decision of every individual was decreed by God, and that, before the foundation of the earth. This reasoning of their logic is required by an a priori presumption that man has no free will and that every soul that gets saved does so because God decreed it, and every soul that gets damned to hell, does so because God decreed it. The whole mislead concept is entangled in their finite concept of God's foreknowledge.

Logically if God foreknows an event, then that event will come to pass; that event cannot be changed by the will of man; that event cannot be changed by the prayers of man; that event cannot be changed by the power of God, it is already decreed by God. That logic forces the Baptist who says "God does not 'choose' who gets saved, God just foreknows who will get saved" into the reformed theology of decrees whereby God, before the foundation of the world, decreed who would get saved. One must be careful of that slippery slope of error.

In our definition and consideration of the foreknowledge of God, therefore, we must be careful to use Scripture definition and God's illustration, not the Reformed Theologians restrictive and fatalistic definition. It must, therefore, remain a general knowledge and not a specific knowledge. It must be limited to the called out specifics and not haplessly applied to every heart beat, sigh and corpuscle of every souls existence.

If God declares "whosoever will may come;" if God allows man a free will to "choose you this day whom ye will serve;" if God gives license to mere humans that "whatsoever ye ask in my name I will do it;" then the 'orthodox' definition of foreknowledge and the 'orthodox' consideration of what is included in God's foreknowledge, must be reconstructed and made to conform to Scripture. So it does. So it must.

---

[41]   Strong, Augustus H., Systematic Theology, Part IV, Chapter III, pp 355-356

Another challenge in considering God's foreknowledge is discovered in consideration of God's omniscience and any temporal restrictions He undertook in offering man their free will. If man is truly given a free will within God's restriction, but outside of his direct control, then God waits, in time, on mans will, decision, and action, before he acts or intervenes. This is clearly seen throughout the Bible and cannot be rationally denied. The theological dilemma that this presents however is insurmountable. The 'Open Theology' [42] movement that recently pursued this vein has put theologians in an open uproar because it upset their finite logical model that God can reel forward and backward in time like we do in watching "It's a Wonderful Life[43]" each Christmas time.

This clear and literal rendering of God's word, whereby He acts based on what man thinks, does and prays, has made God temporal, or restricted to, and restricted in, time, which He, being everlasting, created! This clear and literal understanding of God's word also diminishes our concept of His omniscience in that mans free will puts many of his specific decisions and actions as yet undetermined and thus unknowable. Indeed a proper rendering of Scripture shows that the verses used to support God's omniscience are always given in the present tense. The logic of a theologian is severely challenged by these restrictions. They will insist that God can reel time backward and forward without restriction and that his omniscience is for every moment on His film reel, giving Him complete access to your every decision and direction. This turns foreknowledge into fatalism and Calvinism. The theologian will twist and take out of context (and he has) as many Scriptures as necessary to keep God free to move about in time, and free to foreknow your every pulse and decision, but the Bible does not lock him there. This makes for a controversial standoff between our logic, our free will, and our categorization of God's attributes. The simplest solutions are all cornered, categorized, over simplified, and staunchly defended; i.e. God knows all and chose all, Calvinism; God knows little, chose none and then holds onto none, Arminianism, or Open Theology were God is not omnipresent, just very present, not omniscient just very niscient, not omnipotent, just very potent.

---

[42] The 'Open Theology' movement is dealt with in more depth later in this chapter.

[43] A 1946 Feature Film directed by Frank Capra, with James Stewart, Donna Reed, Lionel Barrymore.

In Scripture, there is precious little indication that God foreknew in time the insignificant details of ones life. In fact we will discover that there are only 5 recorded things revealed that God knew before the foundation of the earth. We must be careful not to add to that list with our finite logic, no matter how sound we consider it. Let the revelation of Scripture determine what God foreknew, not the inevitable finite logic of our theology.

The Quagmire Of Open Theology

Another, more current, 'knee jerk' reaction to the error's of Calvinism and the reformed doctrine of election and predestination of souls, is what is now called 'open theism.' Like Joseph Arminian of 1542, who assembled and published 5 arguments against reformed theology, Richard Rice, (no relation to this author) a follower of Ellen G. White, the Seventh Day Adventist, published arguments against reformed theology in his 1994 book *"The Openness of God: The Relationship of Divine Foreknowledge and Human Free Will.*[44]" Just like reformed theologians of the Presbyterian Church over reacted to Arminian's five arguments with five bold and errant points of Calvinism, now known as TULIP, there is building a large over reaction to Rice's Open Theology. Level heads of Biblical theologians have yet to develop and expound a sound Biblical systematic theology which captures God's emphasis of the free will of man, as well as God's sovereign control and foreknowledge of the events in His universe. Calvinism and Reformed Theology, with its roots in infant baptism, state churches and burning or drowning Anabaptists, is not to be trusted with such a task. Even less could we trust Richard Rice, the Ellenist with roots in Whites' bizarre doctrines of the advents and pitiful doctrine of soteriology. Such a source is not reliable to outline a Biblical solution, but a dialog has been initiated that could produce a healthy alternative to Calvinism and Arminianism when taken in moderation.

Recognize here that this 'movement' arose because current systematic theology works have a blind bias toward reformed theology, with a non personal God who is unable to be influenced by our

---

[44] The Openness of God: A Biblical Challenge to the Traditional Understanding of God (Paperback) by Richard Rice (Author), John Sanders (Author), Clark H. Pinnock (Editor), William Hasker (Contributor) www.amazon.com/Openness-God-Challenge-Traditional-Understanding/dp/0830818529

prayers, unreactive to mans free will decisions, and not responsive to mans independent actions. Until such a work is articulated, one must resolve the very strained understanding in his own mind. This work is but a flag that points out the dilemma, intending to keep you from camping in any of these three corners of Calvinism, Arminianism and now Open Theology. They are each riddled with error and inconsistency. It is currently better to open your Bible and think this out on your own than it is to trust the work of a single theologian writing from his 'camp'. The Reformed Theologian's answers are wholly inadequate, and the buzz of evangelicals reacting to open theology make a good catalyst for a type of independent thinking that keeps one out of the old ruts. (It can also drive us deeper into dead old ruts so that we do not have to think, be careful here, ruts are prevalent.)

Dr. John Sanders has taken up a defense of Open Theology as it has been modified to step out of an errant corner of thinking, back into Biblical light. He provides this partly quoted summary:

> "According to openness theology, the triune God of love has, in almighty power, created all that is and is sovereign over all. In freedom God decided to create beings capable of experiencing his love. In creating us the divine intention was that we would come to experience the triune love and respond to it with love of our own and freely come to collaborate with God towards the achievement of his goals. ...
>
> " Second, God has, in sovereign freedom, decided to make some of his actions contingent upon our requests and actions.... God, at least since creation, experiences duration. God is everlasting through time rather than timelessly eternal.
>
> "Third, the only wise God has chosen to exercise general rather than meticulous providence, allowing space for us to operate and for God to be creative and resourceful in working with us. ... What people do and whether they come to trust God makes a difference concerning what God does-God does not fake the story of human history.
>
> "Fourth, God has granted us the type of freedom (libertarian) necessary for a truly personal relationship of love to develop. Again, this was God's decision, not ours. ...
>
> "Finally, the omniscient God knows all that can be known given the sort of world he created. ... We believe that God could have known every event of the future had God decided to create a fully determined universe. However, in our view God decided to create beings with indeterministic freedom which implies that God chose to create a universe in which the future is not entirely knowable, even for God. ...
>
> "This view may be called dynamic omniscience (it corresponds to the dynamic theory of time rather than the stasis theory). According to this view

God knows the past and present with exhaustive definite knowledge and knows the future as partly definite (closed) and partly indefinite (open)....

" Our rejection of divine timelessness and our affirmation of dynamic omniscience are the most controversial elements in our proposal and the view of foreknowledge receives the most attention. However, the watershed issue in the debate is not whether God has exhaustive definite foreknowledge (EDF) but whether God is ever affected by and responds to what we do. This is the same watershed that divides Calvinism from Arminianism."- Dr. John Sanders[45]

As open theology has been reformed by evangelical scholars it attempts to explain a practical relationship between the free will of man and the sovereignty of God. It clashes with what might be called classical theology where it touches an immutable and timeless God who fully determines the future of man kind. It can go extreme, but taken in moderation, it begins to expose and rectify some of the more obtrusive problems of Reformed Theology and Calvinism. It is still simply a new corner of thinking. Stay out of corners when balancing God's sovereignty with His granting to man free will for decisions. Corners are mentally simple and one can settle in and relax their mind in them, but this is not the time to relax ones mind.

---

[45]   http://www.opentheism.info/ Article by Dr. John Sanders accessed Feb 2007

Chapter 5 Election and Whosoever Will

A first premise for a Biblical doctrine of election and predestination is that man has been given a free will to choose and that this free moral agency can, and is expected by God to make a choice of restoration to his Creator. The Bible teaches that salvation through the atonement of Christ is available and free to every individual, and that every responsible[46] individual has the free will, the moral aptitude, and the moral requirement to accept the redeeming act of the Lord Jesus Christ. No soul can accept this atonement for their sin except the Father draw him (John 6:44[47]), but God is not willing that any should perish (2Pet 3:9[48]) thus God must draw every man to him to be just. He has. God has given each and every man "the True light, which lighteth every man that cometh into the world" (John 1:8-9[49]), "Because that which may be known of God is manifest in them; for God hath shewed it unto them," (Rom 1:18-20[50]) and that "God trieth the hearts and reigns" of every man, to bring them to an acceptance of His free gift of Salvation. (Psalm 7:9, Isa 1:18, Jer 17:10[51])

---

[46] It is readily contended that some mental age of accountability must be attained before a genuine acceptance or rejection of God's atoning offer of his only begotten Son can be transacted. A death prior to this accountability would result in heaven, as it did for David's son. (2Sam 12:23) At the very least it would lean on the question "Shall not the judge of all the earth do right?" (Gen 18:25) A death prior to this accountability horribly confounds and is disingenuous to Calvin's errant doctrine of election.

[47] John 6:44 No man can come to me, except the Father which hath sent me draw him: and I will raise him up at the last day.

[48] 2Pe 3:9 The Lord is not slack concerning his promise, as some men count slackness; but is longsuffering to us-ward, not willing that any should perish, but that all should come to repentance.

[49] John 1:8-9 He was not that Light, but *was sent* to bear witness of that Light. 9 *That* was the true Light, which lighteth every man that cometh into the world.

[50] Rom 1:18 For the wrath of God is revealed from heaven against all ungodliness and unrighteousness of men, who hold the truth in unrighteousness; 19 ¶ Because that which may be known of God is manifest in them; for God hath shewed *it* unto them. 20 For the invisible things of him from the creation of the world are clearly seen, being understood by the things that are made, *even* his eternal power and Godhead; so that they are without excuse:

[51] Psalm 7:9 Oh let the wickedness of the wicked come to an end; but establish the just: for the righteous God trieth the hearts and reins. Isa 1:18 Come now, and let us reason together, saith the LORD: though your sins be as scarlet, they shall be as white as snow; though they be red like crimson, they shall be as wool. Jer 17:10 I the LORD search the heart, *I* try the reins, even to give every man according to his ways, *and* according to the fruit of his doings.

In assembling the Bible doctrine on election a first and foremost consideration must be what the Bible says about the availability of salvation to every man. If God has preordained a few for salvation and the rest for destruction as Calvinism declares because of Augustinian theology, then the offer to the 'whosoevers' of humanity is not valid. A doctrine of election must allow the preponderance of Scriptures which insist on the volitional and moral agency of man. Since the fall in the garden, man attained a "knowledge of good and evil[52]" and the option and ability to choose between the two. The poet puts this truth to prose:

> "See there: - God's signpost standing at the ways
> which every man of his free will must go
> Up the steep hill, or down the winding ways.
> One or the other every man must go.
> He forces no man each must choose his way,
> and as he chooses so his end will be;
> One went in front, to point the perfect way,
> who follows fears not where the end will be.[53]"

Even Marvin R. Vincent, the noted Presbyterian Calvinist acknowledges this truth. In his famous *Word Studies in the New Testament* he writes:

> "That the factor of human economy is too obvious to require reproof. It appears in numerous utterances ... and in the entire drift of Scripture, where man's power of moral choice is both asserted, assumed, and appealed to.[54]"

Those who would study Scripture, even with the blinders of Calvinism in place, see this blatant truth. In *The Philosophy of Christianity* Dr. L.S. Keyer succinctly says:

> "That man has a conscience which distinguishes between right and wrong and a free will by which he is able to choose between them, scarcely seems to require any argument, seeing that he functions in this world as a moral being... His whole experience tells him that he is a free moral being.[55]"

---

[52] Genesis 2:9,17
[53] The Cross and the Crossing by John Onenham (as quoted by Samuel Fisk Chapter 3)
[54] Vincent, Marvin R. *Word Studies in the New Testament* Vol III, p. 136
[55] Keyer, L.S. Dr., *The Philosophy of Christianity* p. 96

Of course a doctrine of election that violates this free-will of man to choose his destiny would make missionary efforts futile. Notice the rigorous attention to this dilemma detailed by Steve R. Morris, Independent Baptist Missionary to Mexico:

> "When God says 'Whosoever will may come...', it means literally what God says. God is making a legitimate offer of salvation to all of mankind. He is not saying what He really does not mean. God can not 'command all men everywhere to repent.' and know that since He has already condemned certain people to hell, and they have no choice in the matter (as Calvinism falsely teaches), and therefore they can not repent. In other words, the Calvinist would say He is not really making a legitimate offer. He is not really saying what He means. No! Salvation is freely offered to all who will repent and believe. All who choose (and this is a key thing, we all have a free will) to repent and receive Christ are the "elect". You have to make a choice "multitudes, multitudes in the valley of decision..." ... God gives us a free will. Otherwise, you could accuse God of being unjust, because if we really have no free will, we are not responsible for our wrong choices."

The major dilemma with the Calvinistic teaching is its elimination of man's free will. Even R.C. Sproul, an avid advocate of 5 point Calvinism[56], when teaching on this subject admitted that he did not have time to address man's free will under this topic and that he could answer no questions about volition of man under his discussion of Augustinian Theology, and Calvinism. He did, however, admit that this was a major issue in the consideration of election.

Thus, whatever election may be, it cannot infringe on this free will choice of man to 'choose you this day whom ye will serve'[57]. In Dr. Alan Richardson's book *An Introduction To The Theology Of The New Testament* there is an extended section on "the elect of God." In his analysis of election in the Old Testament he concludes: "election in the Old Testament is to service of God in this world and has nothing at all to do with salvation in the world to come.[58]" Coming to New Testament terminology he says:

> "A proper understanding of the New Testament doctrine of election in Christ will dispel the somber and frightening mistakes of post reformation theories

---

[56] Audio Series *"Predestination"* by R.C. Sproul from Ligonier Ministries, The Home of *"Renewing Your Mind"* Orlando, FL.
[57] Joshua 24:15
[58] Richardson, Dr. Alan, *An Introduction To The Theology Of The New Testament* p. 272

about predestination, double predestination, reprobation and the rest of the lingering errors of medievalism, from which the rise of Biblical science has happily set us free... Election refers to God's purpose in this world,... In the New Testament, as in the Old Testament, election is a matter of Service, not of privilege[59]"

On Rom 9:14-24 Dr. Richardson writes:

"the passage is not saying anything at all about ultimate salvation in the world to come ... God's salvation itself is unearned, a free gift, so also is the privilege of serving God's purpose as an elected vessel of his design.[60]"

The Scriptures we have already looked at clarify that man must make his own choice because salvation is available to the 'whosoever.' The Calvinist doctrine of unconditional election states that "*God's choice of who to save was made in eternity past and was not conditioned upon man's ability, life acts or future response to God's gracious offer of salvation.*" Such a statement violates a salvation available to 'whosoever believeth.' Scripture declares that every man is given adequate Light to make a choice and is without excuse. This stands in stark contrast to the Calvinist doctrine of total depravity which states "*mans spiritually and totally dead state from the fall affects every area of his life and person wherein he can not even call out to God even as a dead man can not speak.*" Scripture declares that salvation is available to all, i.e. to whosoever will accept it. This stands in stark contrast to the Calvinist errant doctrine of limited atonement which states "*the subjects of Christ's atoning work on the cross are identified as only the elect;...*" Their error continues with the preposterous statement that "*Jesus did not die for all the world; God purposed by the atonement to save only the elect and that consequently all the elect, and they alone, are saved.[61]*" Scripture declares that God is not willing that any should perish but men perish of their own volition. This stands in stark contrast to the Calvinist doctrine of irresistible grace, which states "*the Holy Spirit actually, controllably and supremely brings to salvation all the elect and only the elect.*" In the simple examination of what the Scripture states about the availability of salvation and the volition of man, yeah the obligation of every man to choose for themselves, any Bible student

---

[59] Ibid pp. 274-275
[60] Ibid pp. 280-287
[61] Kuiper, R.B. *For whom Did Christ Die?* p. 62

can bring into question every Calvinist doctrine of election. Here with but a few Scriptures we refute 4 of the 5 Calvinist principles.[62] Their ideas can not coexist with a sound understanding of salvation as portrayed in the doctrine of soteriology, taken directly from Scripture. Scripture which says "Whosoever therefore shall confess me before men, Mt 10:32, Lu 12:8" or "whosoever shall not be offended in me Mt 11:6, Lu 7:23" or "whosoever shall do the will of my Father which is in heaven, Mt 12:50, Mr 3:35" or "whosoever will save his life, Mt 16:25" or "Whosoever therefore shall humble himself, Mt 18:4" or "Whosoever will come after me, Mr 8:34" or "whosoever shall receive me, Mr 9:37, Lu 9:48" or "Whosoever cometh to me, Lu 6:47" or "whosoever drinketh of the water that I shall give him, Joh 4:14" or "whosoever liveth and believeth in me Joh 11:26" or "through his name whosoever believeth in him Ac 10:43, Joh 3:15" or "whosoever believeth on him Ro 9:33, Ro 10:11" or " whosoever believeth on me Joh 12:46" or "whosoever shall call on the name of the Lord shall be saved. Rom 10:13" "For God so loved the world, that he gave his only begotten Son, that whosoever believeth in him should not perish, but have everlasting life." "For whosoever shall call upon the name of the Lord shall be saved." ... "That if thou shalt confess with thy mouth the Lord Jesus, and shalt believe in thine heart that God hath raised him from the dead, thou shalt be saved. For with the heart man believeth unto righteousness; and with the mouth confession is made unto salvation. For the scripture saith, Whosoever believeth on him shall not be ashamed."

Next we will see that no unregenerate man could be elect, for "As it is written, There is none righteous, no, not one: ... For all have sinned, and come short of the glory of God;" (Rom 3:10,23) Consequently, one gets elect only when placed into the only Elect One.

---

[62]   TULIP has as its premise 1)Total Depravity, 2) Unconditional Election, 3) Limited Atonement, 4) Irresistible Grace, 5) Perseverance of the Saints

Chapter 6 Election and the One Elect

A second premise of a Biblical doctrine of election and predestination is that since the saints are addressed as the elect, and the unregenerate sinner is not, there must be a transition between the two, i.e. a time when one becomes an elect one. The Bible teaches that every man is born in sin, born unsaved and unregenerate, (Isa 53:6, Rom 3:10-12,23[63]) and we are establishing that no man is chosen, elected, or predestined towards his soul's salvation. There is *one* man born into this world without sin, the man Christ Jesus. He is the only one elect before the foundation of the world (1Pet 1:20[64]) and He is the only elect one at birth.   He was, of course, elect for the work of redemption, (1Pet 2:4-6[65]) not for individual salvation. Consequently, nowhere in the Bible is any unregenerate human chosen, elected, or predestined to receive the salvation of their soul, (Acts 17:30[66]) and nowhere in the NT is an unregenerate human called 'the elect.' Thus, at no time is man chosen, elected or predestined to enter into Christ or to receive eternal glory in heaven. He must so enter by his own volition, and his own acceptance of the Lord Jesus Christ[67]. (Rom 10:11-13[68]) One only becomes the elect by entering into the Elect One.

---

[63]   Isa 53:6 All we like sheep have gone astray; we have turned every one to his own way; and the LORD hath laid on him the iniquity of us all. Rom 3:10-12 As it is written, There is none righteous, no, not one: 11 There is none that understandeth, there is none that seeketh after God. 12 They are all gone out of the way, they are together become unprofitable; there is none that doeth good, no not one. Rom 3:23 For all have sinned, and come short of the glory of God;

[64]   1Pet 1:20 Who verily was foreordained before the foundation of the world, but was manifest in these last times for you,

[65]   1Pet 2:4-6 ¶ To whom coming, *as unto* a living stone, disallowed indeed of men, but chosen of God, *and* precious, 5 Ye also, as lively stones, are built up a spiritual house, an holy priesthood, to offer up spiritual sacrifices, acceptable to God by Jesus Christ. 6 Wherefore also it is contained in the Scripture, Behold, I lay in Zion a chief corner stone, elect, precious: and he that believeth on him shall not be confounded.

[66]   Acts 17:30 And the times of this ignorance God winked at; but now commandeth all men every where to repent:

[67]   Likewise, at no time is man chosen, elected, or predestined to enter into eternal damnation. He must so enter by his own volition and his own rejection of the Light of God, (John 1:8-9, 3:18-19) and the rejection of God's tug on the reins of his soul. (Psalm 7:9, Isa 1:18, Jer 17:10)

[68]   Rom 10:11-13 For the scripture saith, Whosoever believeth on him shall not be ashamed. 12 ¶ For there is no difference between the Jew and the Greek: for the same Lord over all is rich unto all that call upon him. 13 For whosoever shall call upon the name of the Lord shall be saved.

A foundation stone in understanding the Bible doctrine of election is in the understanding that there is only one elect, foreordained, chosen individual, the man Christ Jesus. Even in his transliterated name, the Christ (Greek), the Messiah (Hebrew) we find He is the 'Anointed One', i.e. Elect. If another human is elect, it is because he is 'in' this Chosen One and partakes in His election. It is not because he was elect any time prior to his entry into Christ. He became elect when placed in Christ and he is placed in Christ by his new birth which made him instantaneously converted, justified, regenerated (or quickened), indwelt by the Spirit and baptized (a Greek transliteration meaning 'immersed') 'in' the Lord Jesus Christ. (Do not equate or confuse the latter with water baptism, the two are completely separate entities.) Now prior to one's salvation, man is neither elect, chosen nor predestined. When one receives salvation they receive all three by virtue of their being 'in' Christ.

This concept has been confused in previous illustrations whereby a sign is posted at the doorway of the Cross of Calvary. The sign says "Whosoever Will" on one side but once passing through that door and looking back at the sign the reverse side says "Elect of God." This illustration can allude that the 'whosoever' was elect all the time, but didn't realize it until the receipt of salvation. No! No! Prior to salvation there is no election or predestination resting on any soul. They inherit their election and predestination with their eternal life that they inherit at their salvation. It all comes in one package.

If one could ever be elect for a salvation experience, then logically that election would take place prior to the foundation of the world, it would be unchangeable, it would seal ones fate, and it would do so even before their conception! That is not found in the Bible. Clearly from the Bible there is

Only One Foreordained before the foundation of the World
"Forasmuch as ye know that ye were not redeemed with corruptible things, *as* silver and gold, from your vain conversation *received* by tradition from your fathers; 19 But with the precious blood of Christ, as of a lamb without blemish and without spot: 20 **Who verily was foreordained before the foundation of the world**, but was manifest in these last times for you, 21 Who by him do believe in God, that raised him up from the dead, and gave him glory; that your faith and hope might be in God." (1Pet 1:18-21, emphasis added) It is quite self explanatory here, that The Lord Jesus Christ is the one 'foreordained before the foundation of the world', not the fate nor destiny of individual souls.

Consider Mt 13:35 "That it might be fulfilled which was spoken by the prophet, saying, I will open my mouth in parables; I will utter things which have been kept secret **from the foundation of the world**." Here, the progressive revelation of God shows there are 'things' kept secret from the foundation of the world, but not elect individuals.

Consider Mt 25:34 "Then shall the King say unto them on his right hand, Come, ye blessed of my Father, inherit the kingdom prepared for you **from the foundation of the world**:" Here it is the 'kingdom prepared' that was from the foundation of the world, again no reference to individuals being selected for that kingdom.

Consider Luke 11:50 "That the blood of all the prophets, which was shed from the foundation of the world, may be required of this generation;" Where 'from the foundation of the world' is indicating 'since the world began,' and is thus another more concrete Greek form of the same.

Consider John 17:24 "Father, I will that they also, whom thou hast given me, be with me where I am; that they may behold my glory, which thou hast given me: for thou lovedst me **before the foundation of the world**." Again it is Christ himself that is referenced as present and loved before the foundation of the world.

Ephesians 1:4 will be carefully considered in the next section but it states: "According as he hath chosen us in him before the foundation of the world, that we should be holy and without blame before him in love:" It is developed in the next section that the 'us' speaks of corporateness not individual election, and the choice is that 'we' who are in Christ should be holy. Even this mainstay of Calvinism does not say individual souls are chosen out before the foundation of the world.

Consider Heb 4:3 "For we which have believed do enter into rest, as he said, As I have sworn in my wrath, if they shall enter into my rest: although the works were finished **from the foundation of the world**." It is awesome here that God references the redeeming work of His only begotten son as though they were finished from the foundation of the world. In His mind they were then finished. The Son was chosen and the work was deemed completed before He said "It is finished," but no reference is made to individuals being selected.

Consider Heb 9:26 "For then must he often have suffered **since the foundation of the world**: but now once in the end of the world hath he appeared to put away sin by the sacrifice of himself." No individual souls are chosen from the foundation of the world in these references. Christ was, and his work was; individual souls were not.

How about 2Ti 2:19 "Nevertheless the **foundation of God** standeth sure, having this seal, The Lord knoweth them that are his. And, Let every one that nameth the name of Christ depart from iniquity." Here there is a solid foundation for what God knows. Clearly here we can see that only those 'that nameth the name of Christ' are His. They were not His before they took His name. When they did they are known to be His; i.e. the knowing of them is not necessarily from the foundation of the world in this sentence, nor did he know them in this sense, before they named the name of Christ.

But what of Rev13:8 "And all that dwell upon the earth shall worship him, whose names are not written in the book of life of the Lamb slain **from the foundation of the world**." Clearly here the foundation of the world found the Lamb slain, but not necessarily the book written. Likewise in Rev 17:8 "The beast that thou sawest was, and is not; and shall ascend out of the bottomless pit, and go into perdition: and they that dwell on the earth shall wonder, whose names were not written in the book of life **from the foundation of the world**, when they behold the beast that was, and is not, and yet is." Here we can see that this book of God's record keeping existed, but it was not completely written, at the foundation of the world.

There are a total of eight references to this 'book of life'[69] in the Bible. Its existence has been interpreted in three ways 1) that it contains the names of those who are elect for salvation from the foundation of the earth (one can guess from previous discussion that this Biblical understanding of election will cause rejection of that interpretation.) 2) that it contains the names of all humans and those who reject Christ and then die have their names blotted out. This view springs from an idea that none of the 8 references seem to indicate the writing of new names into the book, while some talk of blotting names out, and it nicely covers a consideration of those who never reach an 'age of accountability.'[70] And lastly, 3) that as one is born again God writes his name in the book and there is now "a new name written down in glory" as the song writer aptly expressed it.

Where it touches this doctrinal analysis the only problematic verse could be Rev 17:8. In order to fit well with our systematic analysis of election so far it is preferred that Rev 17:8 be read as a

---

[69] 'book of life' referenced in Php 4:3, Rev 3:5, 13:8, 17:8, 20:12, 15, 21:27, and 22:19

[70] The Bible does not speak of an 'age of accountability.' The concept is devised in the mind of man to help account that David said he would go to his infant son (in heaven), but also account that all who die without Christ are cast away from God.

reference to the book that existed before the foundation of the world as mentioned in Rev 13:8 and not as a book of pre-written names existing before the foundation of the world. Thus the book existed from the foundation of the world, but the names are written in or blotted out as a matter of God's real time record keeping, not as a pre-written fatalist description of who would get in. Some extend God's foreknowledge to a level of knowing man's individual choices. When taking this man made extension of God's foreknowledge, they try to say that it is still in no way causative. Even using God's non-causative foreknowledge to interpret Rev 17:8 with a pre-written book of life, containing preselected names who would receive God's grace is dangerously fatalistic with insufficient room for God's "*whosoever will may come.*" (We shall establish in chapter 10 that extending God's foreknowledge to every infinite detail of future events or decision of man, is without Scriptural basis and grossly restricts mans free will) Thus Rev 17:8 is interpreted as having a "book of life from the foundation of the world" with names being written in and blotted from as time goes on, as indicated in other Scriptures.Notice also the context of this reference is talking about the tribulation saints, (or in this case particularly those who are not the saints) saints which do not get into heaven in the dispensation of grace as the Church, the body of Christ, but saints who are won to Christ in the tribulation period.These saints are treated differently in Scripture than those won to Christ and added to his Church during the pre-rapture dispensational age of grace.

A couple other verses mention things existing 'before the world'. These are examined as follows:

John 17:5 "And now, O Father, glorify thou me with thine own self with the glory which I had with thee **before the world was.**" Again, the everlasting glory of God was present before the world.

1Co 2:7 "But we speak the wisdom of God in a mystery, *even* the hidden *wisdom*, which God ordained **before the world** unto our glory:" Again Proverbs 8 and this verse contend that God's wisdom was present before the world.

2Ti 1:9 "Who hath saved us, and called *us* with an holy calling, not according to our works, but according to his own purpose and grace, which was given us in Christ Jesus **before the world began,**" Here, the purpose of God and the grace of God were both given in Christ Jesus before the world began. Notice they were given 'in Christ Jesus' not given to us before the world. For you or I to receive this calling, this purpose, and this grace, we need to be 'in Christ' where they have long been located. This is good soteriology.

Tit 1:2 "In hope of eternal life, which God, that can not lie, promised **before the world began;**" As much as his wisdom was present, and his Son was present, and his plan to send his redeeming were present, so too was the hope and promise of eternal life present before the world began.

Thus the only Bible verse that may be problematic for the harmony of this doctrine of election is Rev 17:8, and this reference is clearly speaking of tribulation saints, and of a book of life that existed (not completely written) before the foundation of the world. The preponderance of other Scriptures require that the interpretation of this single verse be conformed to the majority. And this explanation does not hinder the understanding and clear indication that God did not pre-ordain some souls to be saved and some to be lost. He only pre-ordained His Only Begotten Son, and him slain from the foundation of the world. We thus become elect, chosen and predestined by being placed 'in' the only Elect One.

Chapter 7 Election and the Elect Ones

The Bible is clear in the NT references that 'the elect', 'the chosen', and 'the predestined' are those who are 'in Christ' with out reference made to the free-will decision that positioned them 'in Christ'; and that their now being 'in Christ' is what makes them 'the elect,'[71] as part of the corporate body in Christ, (Rom 8:33, Col 3:12, 2John 1:1 ,13, 1Pet 5:13[72]); it makes them 'the chosen'[73] for sanctification, holiness, witness and service in His name (Luke 6:13, Eph 1:4, Acts 9:5, 1Thes 1:4[74]); and it makes them 'the predestined'[75] elect who will be conformed to the image of his Son. (Rom 8:29-30[76]) Thus, men are not chosen to be in Christ, but by virtue of their being in Christ they become 'the elect', as He was, and is, The Elect; they become 'the chosen' as He was, and is, The Chosen; and they, by virtue of their being in Christ, are now 'predestined' to be conformed to His image and His purposes.

To examine this statement one should examine every occurrence of these words in the New Testament. Before doing that it will be helpful to get a good definition for 'corporate.' To counter the obvious error of an individual soul's election for salvation some have promoted a 'corporate election' solution for every occurrence of these 3 terms. Such a solution will be shown barely suitable but it is far better than the error of Calvinism, wherein individual souls are elected for

---

[71] Greek εκλεκτο & συνεκλεκτο J. Strong Concordance #1588, & #4899

[72] Rom 8:33 Who shall lay any thing to the charge of God's elect? *It is* God that justifieth. Col 3:12 ¶ Put on therefore, as the elect of God, holy and beloved, bowels of mercies, kindness, humbleness of mind, meekness, longsuffering; 2John 1:1 ¶ The elder unto the elect lady and her children, whom I love in the truth; and not I only, but also all they that have known the truth;... 13 The children of thy elect sister greet thee. Amen. 1Pet 5:13 The *church that is* at Babylon, elected together with *you,* saluteth you; and so *doth* Marcus my son.

[73] Greek εκλεγομαι & εκλογη J. Strong Concordance #1586, & #1589

[74] Luke 6:13 And when it was day, he called *unto him* his disciples: and of them he chose twelve, whom also he named apostles; Eph 1:4 According as he hath chosen us in him before the foundation of the world, that we should be holy and without blame before him in love: Acts 9:5 And he said, Who art thou, Lord? And the Lord said, I am Jesus whom thou persecutest: *it is* hard for thee to kick against the pricks. 1Thes 1:4 Knowing, brethren beloved, your election of God.

[75] Greek προοριζω, J. Strong Concordance #4309

[76] Rom 8:29 ¶ For whom he did foreknow, he also did predestinate *to be* conformed to the image of his Son, that he might be the firstborn among many brethren. 30 Moreover whom he did predestinate, them he also called: and whom he called, them he also justified: and whom he justified, them he also glorified.

salvation before birth and then regenerated before conversion! In the Biblical doctrine of election there is no individual selection for salvation, however, there is often a corporateness in the use of these Bible terms, and Christians are 'corporate' by definition.

> **"cor·po·rate** (kôr′pər-ĭt, kôr′prĭt) *adj.* **1.** Formed into a corporation; incorporated. **2.** Of or relating to a corporation: *corporate assets; corporate culture.* **3. United or combined into one body; collective:** *made a corporate effort to finish the job.* **4.** Corporative. [Latin *corporātus*, past participle of *corporāre*, to make into a body, from *corpus*, body. See **kwrep-** below.] **--cor′po·rate·ly** *adv.*
>
> **cor·po·ra·tion** (kôr′pə-rā′shən) *n. Abbr.* **corp. 1.** A body that is granted a charter legally recognizing it as a separate legal entity having its own rights, privileges, and liabilities distinct from those of its members. **2.** Such a body created for purposes of government. Also called body corporate. **3. A group of people combined into or acting as one body**.[77]"

Obviously our salvation is an act that makes us "United or combined into one body," as in both definitions #3 above. We are put into the body of Christ and are thus, now a corporation. In exegesis the treatment of terms 'elect', 'chosen' and 'predestined' easily falls into this corporate provision. Being 'in Christ' makes you part of the body of Christ and this body is 'elect'; this body is 'chosen'; this body is 'predestined' corporately. In any instances where an individual election could be considered it is important to see that there is no exegetical room for being elect for salvation into Christ, only being elected because one is 'in Christ.'

With that as a backdrop let's examine every occasion of the words 'elect', 'chosen' and 'predestined' in the New Testament. This may seem tedious but should be undertaken for completeness. First let's examine the word 'choose'. Most clearly showing its meaning in the Luke 6:13 reference,

And of them he *chose* (εκλεγομαι)[78] twelve

---

[77] The American Heritage Dictionary of the English Language, Third Edition.

[78] There are those who object to the use of both the Greek language and Strong's numeric annotations in this study, considering it a slander against the accuracy of the King James English translation. It is not that, the author holds more strongly to the accuracy of the Authorized Version than they, even because of his limited Greek learning. The thorough examinations of these terms is only enabled by the use of the Greek language and Strong's numbers. Please be patient with each.

First, the word: **Choose** Strong's Concordance[79] Number 1586, εκλεγομαι or eklegomai is pronounced *ek-leg'-om-ahee.*   It is a verb; translated 21 times in New Testament as 'choose' 19 times, 'choose out', 1 time, and 'make choice' 1 time for the 21 total usages. Definition: εκλεγομαι Choose out; to pick out, choose, to pick or choose out for one's self a) choosing one out of many, i.e. Jesus choosing his disciples b) choosing one for an office.

The first use of this word #1586, εκλεγομαι, is found in Mar 13:20 as follows: "And except that the Lord had shortened those days, no flesh should be saved: but for the elect's sake, whom he hath chosen <1586>, he hath shortened the days." Here, the context is the tribulation period that is to be upon the earth, and the word, chosen, clarifies who 'the elect' are. These are saints, i.e. saved ones, in the tribulation period, who are thus not technically part of the Church, which was previously raptured (1Thes 4). (Although not technically part of the Church they are saints that are to be part of the first resurrection according to Rev 20:5-6) In our previous introduction to these saints we have seen that Scripture often treats these saints differently than those saved and made part of the pre-rapture body of Christ. In our study here, we note that it is a reference to those who are saved, not a reference to any who are to get saved in the future. Thus the chosen in Mar 13:20 are not chosen for salvation, but chosen for service because they are clearly already 'in Christ.'

A second use of the word #1586, εκλεγομαι, is: Luk 6:13 "And when it was day, he called *unto him* his disciples: and of them he chose <1586> twelve, whom also he named apostles;" Here again, the chosen are not chosen out of the unsaved masses of mankind, they are not chosen for salvation, but chosen from amongst the disciples for service. Thus the chosen in Luke 6:13 are not chosen for salvation, but chosen for service because they are, at this point, the followers of Christ. Recall that one of them is Judas.

The third and forth use of word #1586, εκλεγομαι, are: Luk 10:42 "But one thing is needful: and Mary hath chosen <1586> that good part, which shall not be taken away from her. And Luk 14:7 And he put forth a parable to those which were bidden, when he marked how they chose out <1586> the chief rooms; saying unto them," In these two verses we see

[79] Strong, James J. S.T.D., L.L.D., *The Exhaustive Concordance of the Bible: Showing Every Word of the Test of the Common English Version of the Canonical Books*

51

man doing the choosing. This is not germane to our examination except to understand better the usage of this word throughout the Scriptures.

The 5th and 6th use of word# 1586, εκλεγομαι, are: John 6:70 "Jesus answered them, Have not I chosen <1586> you twelve, and one of you is a devil?" And John 13:18 "I speak not of you all: I know whom I have chosen <1586>: but that the scripture may be fulfilled, He that eateth bread with me hath lifted up his heel against me." In John we have four references dealing with the choosing of the twelve. Clearly, in chapter 6 and 13 Judas was one of the chosen twelve. But Judas was not chosen for eternal salvation, clearly he was chosen for service, that the Scripture would be fulfilled. Was Judas then chosen for eternal destruction? No! Judas was chosen for service in the Kingdom of God, even though, in the end he did not apparently become a part of the Kingdom of God. Judas is an example of one who was 'chosen' but likely did not receive salvation. Such salvation was available to him, he could have made a volitional choice to believe and receive the Christ. Yeah he, who saw the miracles, and did the miracles with Christ, of all people, should have believed in the Saviour. In the end, it appears he did not, but God used him just the same, and in the end used him as the betrayer. We find in Judas, then a curious 'election.' He was not a believer, and thus not part of the elect body of Christ, and not called the elect. Indeed in these two verses it is pointed out clearly that though Judas was chosen for service, he was not "in Christ" and thus was never referred to as elect. In order to be elect you must be "in Christ."

Use number 8 and 9 of word# 1586, εκλεγομαι, are: John 15:16 "Ye have not chosen <1586> me, but I have chosen <1586> you, and ordained you, that ye should go and bring forth fruit, and *that* your fruit should remain: that whatsoever ye shall ask of the Father in my name, he may give it you. And John 15:19 If ye were of the world, the world would love his own: but because ye are not of the world, but I have chosen <1586> you out of the world, therefore the world hateth you." In John 15 we see the disciples being 'chosen' linked with their being 'ordained.' Because of their being chosen they do not fit into this world. Notice here the difference between choosing and ordaining. It is the difference between selecting and investing with authority. Clearly the two are linked here, the chosen, as we have stated are invested with authority because they are given a task to do in this life. Clearly, again this election has to do with their service not the salvation of the soul. Thus the chosen in

John 6, 13 and 15 are not chosen for their eternal salvation, but chosen specifically for tasks that Christ wanted performed here on this earth.

The 10th through the 16th use of word# 1586, εκλεγομαι, are found in Acts as follows: Acts 1:2 "Until the day in which he was taken up, after that he through the Holy Ghost had given commandments unto the apostles whom he had chosen <1586>:" Notice here the apostles were chosen for service.

Acts 1:24 "And they prayed, and said, Thou, Lord, which knowest the hearts of all *men*, shew whether of these two thou hast chosen <1586>," Notice here they were chosen for service.

Acts 6:5 "And the saying pleased the whole multitude: and they chose <1586> Stephen, a man full of faith and of the Holy Ghost, and Philip, and Prochorus, and Nicanor, and Timon, and Parmenas, and Nicolas a proselyte of Antioch: " Notice here they were chosen for service.

Acts 13:17 "The God of this people of Israel chose <1586> our fathers, and exalted the people when they dwelt as strangers in the land of Egypt, and with an high arm brought he them out of it." Notice here the fathers of Israel were chosen for service.

Acts 15:7 "And when there had been much disputing, Peter rose up, and said unto them, Men and brethren, ye know how that a good while ago God made choice <1586> among us, that the Gentiles by my mouth should hear the word of the gospel, and believe." Notice here the Gentiles were chosen corporately not individually.

Acts 15:22 "Then pleased it the apostles and elders, with the whole church, to send chosen <1586> men of their own company to Antioch with Paul and Barnabas; *namely*, Judas surnamed Barsabas, and Silas, chief men among the brethren:" Notice here they were chosen for service.

Acts 15:25 "It seemed good unto us, being assembled with one accord, to send chosen <1586> men unto you with our beloved Barnabas and Paul," Notice here they were chosen for service.

Upon examination of every reference in the book of Acts which uses the word εκλεγομαι <1586> you see that there is not one reference to being chosen for individual salvation. In Acts 15:7 there are those chosen to hear the gospel and we must reiterate that the Gentiles were chosen corporately to be recipients of the gospel, God speaks of this corporate choosing in the Old Testament. (Isa 11:10; 42:1,6; 49:6,22; 60:3,5, 11) Every other usage in the book has to do with being chosen for service. Note that in Acts 13:17 the choosing is towards the fathers of Israel, and we have already demonstrated that such choosing was not towards salvation of the soul but towards the tasks set before a chosen people. Thus the 'chosen' in the book of Acts are not chosen for their eternal salvation. Upon going through half of the New Testament with this word study there is a precedence being set that must be weighed into the use of this word through the epistles. That precedence is that God's choosing is not about salvation but about service. Let's then follow this word through the epistles.

The 17th, 18th and 19th use of the word# 1586, εκλεγομαι, is in Paul's first letter to Corinth: 1Co 1:27 "But God hath chosen <1586> the foolish things of the world to confound the wise; and God hath chosen <1586> the weak things of the world to confound the things which are mighty;" And 1Co 1:28 "And base things of the world, and things which are despised, hath God chosen <1586>, yea, and things which are not, to bring to nought things that are:" Should one take these references in Paul's letter to Corinth to mean a choosing for receipt of salvation, one would be sloppy in their exegesis. Clearly it is our election to be His witnesses, our ordaining to be heralds of the gospel that is in direct view with this usage. Calvinists avoid this letter to Corinth while they develop the exegetical fog around their theology.

The 20th use of word# 1586, εκλεγομαι, is a Calvinist favorite found in: Eph 1:4 "According as he hath chosen <1586> us in him before the foundation of the world, that we should be holy and without blame before him in love:" If there is any meat on the bones of the Calvinists theology they try to develop it here in Ephesians 1. In this Scripture however, we see the language of corporate election, not an individual soul's selection for salvation. Also in Ephesians 1:5, and 11 we see the explanation of our predestination which is also in this corporate sense.

Miss impressions men start with are often hard to shake off. One knows and teaches that Noah's Ark landed on Mt. Ararat, but it takes great effort to say that the kangaroo and platypus 1st came from the Middles East, having been taught otherwise from youth. Here in Ephesians chapter 1 one can state that every chosen and predestined soul is already found 'in Christ', before they can be called 'chosen' or 'predestinated,' but a predisposition about election will require that they say that several times and that they consciously dismiss what many have been taught from childhood. Some will refuse this transition, but this seed of truth, planted in a fertile spirit and watered by much Bible reading will grow to fruition.

In verse 4 we see that the 'us' that were chosen before the foundation of the world are those that make it into Christ by volitional faith (the only way in), and thus, this corporate collection of believers 'in him' were chosen to be holy and without blame before him in love.

This is not individuals who are chosen for salvation before the foundation of the world as the Calvinist's have taught us from our youth. Corporate election exactly fits this context. Remember that this is Paul's introductory material which is to be fully developed in subsequent chapters. In those chapters Paul makes known the 'mystery' "that the Gentiles should be fellowheirs and of the same body, and partakers of his promise in Christ by the gospel;" (Eph 3:6) This is clearly a case of corporate election, and so is Ephesians 1:3-14. That these new Gentile believers at Ephesus, by virtue of their being 'in Christ', were as chosen as anybody, is the context of Paul's challenge to them that they "walk worthy of the vocation wherewith ye are called." It is a vocation wherewith they are called not a salvation wherewith they are called. What is the vocation wherewith they were called? They are now 'in the body' that was chosen and they need to so walk. Ephesians 1:3-14 demands a non Calvinist reading in view of the whole context of the epistle. Doing so clearly brings out the corporateness of the choosing and the predestination. The corporate body of those 'in Christ' are chosen "before the foundation of the world, that we should be holy and without blame before him in love, having predestinated us unto the adoption of children by Jesus Christ to himself, according to the good pleasure of his will." (verse 1:4-5) This is not to be read as individual selection of some to be saved and some to be lost. This is clearly a use of election and predestination in the corporate sense. The Calvinist has argued this Scripture as the clearest teaching of their errant doctrine. But in so doing they must completely leave the clear context of these Scriptures. The context is our walk in Christ not our coming to Christ. The context is what God the Father has done (1:3-6) to the praise of the glory of His grace; what God the Son has done (1:7-12) to the praise of His glory; and what God the Spirit has done (1:13-14) unto the praise of His glory. Therefore walk worthy of the **vocation** wherewith ye are called.

Lastly for the 21st use of the word εκλεγομαι <1586> we find: James 2:5 "Hearken, my beloved brethren, Hath not God chosen <1586> the poor of this world rich in faith, and heirs of the kingdom which he hath promised to them that love him?" At this point in our word study it should be easy to see that the chosen in James 2:5 are not chosen for the receipt of salvation, not chosen to be the sole recipients of eternal life, but chosen because they are 'in Christ', chosen because they are "them that love him." In context this is given in a lesson against shewing favoritism toward the rich. Strange that man's theories should turn its use towards the favoritism of the Calvinist's 'elect for salvation.' This is clearly, not the intent of James.

In the examination of all 21 usages of the word 'chosen', word #1586, εκλεγομαι, there is not one instance where individual souls were chosen for salvation. Each use has to do with choosing for service in the Kingdom of God here on this earth and in this life.

Another word study in order here is the use of the word, εκλεκτοσ Strong number 1588, used 23 times in the New Testament.

The word "Elect"

Strong #1588, εκλεκτοσ eklektos *ek-lek-tos'* is derived from our previous word #1586 εκλεγομαι. It is translated 23 times in New Testament as -elect 16 times, and as chosen 7 times. In definition εκλεκτοσ elect, means simply picked out, or chosen.

The first 10 uses of word #1588 are in the Gospels as follows:

Mt 20:16 "So the last shall be first, and the first last: for many be called, but few chosen <1588>." (The chosen here are those who are 'in Christ')

Mt 22:14 "For many are called, but few *are* chosen <1588>." (The chosen here are those 'in Christ')

Mt 24:22 "And except those days should be shortened, there should no flesh be saved: but for the elect's sake <1588> those days shall be shortened. (The elect here are those 'in Christ')

Mt 24:24 For there shall arise false Christs, and false prophets, and shall shew great signs and wonders; insomuch that, if *it were* possible, they shall deceive the very elect <1588>." (The elect here are those 'in Christ')

Mt 24:31 "And he shall send his angels with a great sound of a trumpet, and they shall gather together his elect <1588> from the four winds, from one end of heaven to the other." (The elect here are those 'in Christ')

Mr 13:20 "And except that the Lord had shortened those days, no flesh should be saved: but for the elect's sake <1588>, whom he hath chosen, he hath shortened the days." (Again, the elect here are those who are 'in Christ')

Mr 13:22 "For false Christs and false prophets shall rise, and shall shew signs and wonders, to seduce, if *it were* possible, even the elect <1588>." (The elect here are those 'in Christ')

Mr 13:27 "And then shall he send his angels, and shall gather together his elect <1588> from the four winds, from the uttermost part of the earth to the uttermost part of heaven." (The elect here are those 'in Christ')

Luk 18:7 "And shall not God avenge his own elect <1588>, which cry day and night unto him, though he bear long with them?" (The elect here are those 'in Christ')

Luk 23:35 "And the people stood beholding. And the rulers also with them derided *him,* saying, He saved others; let him save himself, if he be Christ, the chosen <1588> of God." (The chosen here is in mocking reference to Jesus being the Christ.)

The use of the word throughout the gospels clearly mandates the understanding that the 'elect' are those who are in Christ and not inclusive of those who have not yet received Christ. Again enhancing the doctrine that you only become elect by entering into Christ, and that by volitional faith. None of these verses can dictate that the elect are elect prior to their salvation. Notice in this usage that all the called are not elect, i.e. Some did not enter into Christ, even though they were called. The last verse makes reference that the Christ was supposed to be 'The Elect,' The Christ, The Messiah, the 'Anointed One.' He was 'The Elect', and we note again that we become the elect when we enter into 'The Elect', and not until.

Use number 11, 12 and 13 of word *elect* #1588 are:
Rom 8:33 "Who shall lay any thing to the charge of God's elect <1588>? *It is* God that justifieth".(God's elect have already been justified by declaration, that's salvation, here God justifies them of any charges of late, that is after their salvation.)
Rom 16:13 "Salute Rufus chosen <1588> in the Lord, and his mother and mine." (Rufus is not saluted because of his salvation, but because of his service, we are chosen for service not for salvation!)
Col 3:12 "Put on therefore, as the elect <1588> of God, holy and beloved, bowels of mercies, kindness, humbleness of mind, meekness, longsuffering;" (We were not elect before salvation, but now that we are there are some things that we should put on.)

The use of the word 'elect' in these 3 verses again augments the understanding that the 'elect' are those who are in Christ, and not inclusive of those who have not yet received Christ. Again enhancing the doctrine that you only become elect by entering into Christ, and you only enter into Christ by volitional faith.

The 14th and 15th use of *elect* #1588 are in letters to Timothy:
1Ti 5:21 "I charge *thee* before God, and the Lord Jesus Christ, and the elect <1588> angels, that thou observe these things without preferring one before another, doing nothing by partiality."

Here the use of the 'elect' towards the angels falls into line with the doctrine that the elect are chosen for service not chosen for salvation. Angels have no salvation available to them.
2Ti 2:10 "Therefore I endure all things for <1588> the elect's <1588> sakes, that they may also obtain the salvation which is in Christ Jesus with eternal glory."

This may seem to be our first problem verse for 'ek-lek-tos' with this doctrine. Notice that in this rendering, however, the elect are the 'corporate elect' as used previously by Paul. Rendered in that way Paul endures for the 'body of Christ', that 'they', the unsaved, may be added to the body of the elect. Paul is persuading them to be placed in Christ, not because of their election but by their volition. At any rate the emphasis of this portion of Scripture is on the striving, the laboring and the enduring for the gospel's sake, not on an idea that there are 'elect' out there who still need to be saved. We shall not surrender it willingly but the Calvinist's have used the context of 'the elect' here to allude to the possibility that some 'elect' have not yet attained salvation. The preferred rendering is that there are some individuals out there who, gone after with tears and endurance, would become part of the elect, thus we should strive, labor and endure for the elect's sake.

The 16th and 17th use of word# 1588 are:

Tit 1:1 "Paul, a servant of God, and an apostle of Jesus Christ, according to the faith of God's elect <1588>, and the acknowledging of the truth which is after godliness;"

1Pet 1:2 "Elect <1588> according to the foreknowledge of God the Father, through sanctification of the Spirit, unto obedience and sprinkling of the blood of Jesus Christ: Grace unto you, and peace, be multiplied."

In these two verses we see the 'elect' referenced again in the corporate sense. This especially clarifies Peter's usage here. Those 'in Christ' are elect because of the corporate position in him, and that corporate position was in the foreknowledge of God. Individual decisions for salvation are not found in the foreknowledge of God in this reference. Chapter 10 of this paper deals more with God's foreknowledge. What is found here in the foreknowledge of God, is the existence of a body of believers called the 'elect.'

The 18th, 19th and 20th use of word# 1588 are also found in Peter's 1st Epistle:

1Pet 2:4 "To whom coming, as *unto* a living stone, disallowed indeed of men, but chosen <1588> of God, *and* precious,"

1Pet 2:6 "Wherefore also it is contained in the scripture, Behold, I lay in Sion a chief corner stone, elect <1588>, precious: and he that believeth on him shall not be confounded."

In these two verses of Peter the 'elect' is clearly used for 'The Elect One' the Lord Jesus Christ. We gain our 'elect' status by entering into 'The Elect One', not from a predestined selection of a few for salvation.

1Pet 2:9 "But ye *are* a chosen <1588> generation, a royal priesthood, an holy nation, a peculiar people; that ye should shew forth the praises of him who hath called you out of darkness into his marvellous light:"

Clearly here the corporate election of the saints in this verse is compared to the corporate election of Israel. As Israel was chosen for a particular mission and called upon to be a peculiar people, so too, those who are 'in Christ' are chosen for a particular mission and called upon to be a peculiar people. Not chosen for a salvation experience, chosen for service.

The last three uses of 1588 are by the apostle John:

2John 1:1 "The elder unto the elect <1588> lady and her children, whom I love in the truth; and not I only, but also all they that have known the truth;"
2John 1:13 "The children of thy elect <1588> sister greet thee. Amen."

The Apostle John here is addressing the believer, those who have already come to Christ, not those who are yet unsaved. Thus he calls them the elect, for they are 'in Christ', they are 'in The Elect One.' Clearly this is also the case in the last use of the word 'elect' in Rev 17:14.

Rev 17:14 "These shall make war with the Lamb, and the Lamb shall overcome them: for he is Lord of lords, and King of kings: and they that are with him *are* called, and chosen <1588>, and faithful."

Election used as a Noun

Now seven times the word election is found in the New Testament as a noun. Again do not mind the Greek verbiage if you are not of mind to use it, but it is included here to ensure completeness in the discovery of each usage. Because J. Strong learned to speak Reformed Augustinian very well, let us examine each usage but ignore his Calvinistic Lexicon definition of:

Election

1589 εκλογη ekloge *ek-log-ay'* from 1586 εκλεγομαι ; noun; translated 7 times in the New Testament as -election 6, chosen 1; 7 total

Definition – εκλογη election

1) the act of picking out, choosing
2) a thing or person chosen (edited from *J. Strong's Exhaustive Concordance*)

The first occurrence of the word #1589, εκλογη, is found in:

Acts 9:15 "But the Lord said unto him, Go thy way: for he is a chosen <1589> vessel unto me, to bear my name before the Gentiles, and kings, and the children of Israel:"

Clearly here Paul was not chosen for salvation but for service as has always been the use of the term. There will be those who argue that he must have been chosen before the Damascus road experience, some will argue he was chosen before the foundation of the world, but this is conjecture which is not borne out in the text. Here, in Acts 9:15, Paul was a chosen vessel after he was born-again and in-Christ.

Look now at some verses in Rom 9-11 where Paul expresses his burden that Israel be saved, and reasons about God's grace and fairness toward His people, chosen for service, NOT for salvation.

Rom 9:11 "(For *the children* being not yet born, neither having done any good or evil, that the purpose of God according to election <1589> might stand, not of works, but of him that calleth;)"
Rom 11:5 "Even so then at this present time also there is a remnant according to the election <1589> of grace."
Rom 11:7 "What then? Israel hath not obtained that which he seeketh for; but the election <1589> hath obtained it, and the rest were blinded"
Rom 11:28 "As concerning the gospel, *they are* enemies for your sakes: but as touching the election <1589>, *they are* beloved for the fathers' sakes."

Chapter 13 of this book deals extensively with these verses, but consider here the theme of this section of Scripture. Paul is expressing his concern that God's chosen people, chosen for service (Rom 9:4), chosen as the seed of Christ (Rom 9:5), are missing out on salvation (Rom 9:32). The Israelites system of works and service was blinding them from the free grace of God. This dilemma is the theme of these three chapters. It does not seem fair that corporate Israel, God's 'elect' for service would reject 'so great salvation' and Paul wrestles with this but remains firm"O man, who art thou that repliest against God?", vrs 20. The election contained in this section is continually in reference to the Old Testament election of the Jews and never for their election toward eternal salvation. In fact the troubling theme of this section is that the Old Testament elect do not accept this eternal salvation. Chapter 10 follows up with the clearest verses ever penned about this eternal salvation being available to the 'whosoever' of verse 11 and verse 13.

Rom 10:11 "For the scripture saith, Whosoever believeth on him shall not be ashamed. ... 13 For whosoever shall call upon the name of the Lord shall be saved."

Back in chapter 9 Paul argues "What shall we say then? That the Gentiles, which followed not after righteousness, have attained to righteousness, even the righteousness which is of faith. But Israel, which followed after the law of righteousness, hath not attained to the law of righteousness" Rom 9:30-31. This is Paul's dilemma in this section and it brings out very powerfully that election is for service not for salvation. There is a whole chapter to follow dedicated to examining

Romans chapter 9. New Testament election here is for saints for service to their new King, not for sinners for repentance, because "God is not willing that any should perish" and "whosoever will may come". When they come, they will be part of the New Testament elect, and should an Israelite come, as Paul's heart throb sounds in these chapters, they will also be part of the New Testament elect in Christ. Twice blessed as it were, to be the elect for service of the Old Testament and to be the elect for service of the New Testament. "For the scripture saith, Whosoever believeth on him shall not be ashamed. For there is no difference between Jew and Greek: ... For whosoever shall call upon the name of the Lord shall be saved." Rom 10:11-13

Now let's look at the last two occurrences of word #1589, εκλογη, the noun 'election:'

1Th 1:4 "Knowing, brethren beloved, your election <1589> of God." Notice in 1Thes 1, Paul is addressing the labour of believers when he brings up the election of these saints. They are not elect for salvation, they are elect for service.

2Pe 1:10 "Wherefore the rather, brethren, give diligence to make your calling and election <1589> sure: for if ye do these things, ye shall never fall:"

Again it is clear that the calling and election in this section of Scripture are to service not to salvation. Notice in verse 5-7 the saints are to add to their faith, virtue and knowledge etc. In all these uses of the word 'election', whether in verb or noun, it is never talking about election for salvation. It is ever about election for service. Clearly this is the theme of election throughout the book, there is no election for individual salvation found in the Bible, only in the theology books tainted by Augustinian and Calvinistic doctrines. Learning not to speak Reformed Augustinian involves recognizing where this error has crept into our thinking and being careful to distinguish what the Bible actually says.

One last use of the word as an adjective and our examination of the term is complete.

Elected an Adjective

4899 συνεκλεκτοσ suneklektos *soon-ek-lek-tos'* from a compound of 4862 συν and 1586 εκλεγομαι; adj; translated 1 times in the New Testament as - elected together.

Definition συνεκλεκτοσ Elected together with

1) elected or chosen together with (from *J. Strong's Exhaustive Concordance*)

Here is the use of word# 4899, elected as an adjective:

1Pet 5:13 "The *church that is* at Babylon, elected together with <u><4899></u> *you*, saluteth you; and *so doth* Marcus my son."

      Clearly, here the elect are the church, the church are the saints and the saints are all 'in-Christ' and called to service. There is no Scripture that alludes to an unsaved person being elect toward salvation. The thought of election for salvation has been planted in minds by years of reformed Augustinian thinking. It is errant theological thinking not Bible thinking. In the New Testament of the Holy Bible only those who enter the kingdom are elect, and no one is elect to enter the kingdom. To get into the kingdom, one will have to be a 'whosoever will' and make a voluntary, noncompulsory, free will decision to convert to Christ. If you have not, you surely need to, for the Bible says "He that hath the Son hath life; *and* he that hath not the Son of God hath not life." (1John 5:12) and that "He that believeth on the Son hath everlasting life: and he that believeth not the Son shall not see life; but the wrath of God abideth on him." (John 3:36)

Chapter 8 Election and the Predestined

The Bible teaches that those incorporated into the body of Christ by their faith, conversion, and new birth, are necessarily predestined "to be conformed to the image of (God's) Son," (Rom 8:29) and being sealed by the Holy Spirit of God this destiny is certain. (2Cor 1:22) This destiny of the believers was predetermined by God. In the Scriptures, 'which' individuals would believe was not predetermined, but that 'the believers' would be conformed to Christ was predetermined. This predetermination is completely in the corporate sense.

Let's simply do an examination of what the Bible says; there are six uses of the word:

Predestinate

J. Strongs word# 4309 προοριζω proorizo *pro-or-id'-zo* from 4253 προ and 3724 οριζω ; verb.

It is translated 6 times in the New Testament as -predestinate 4 times, as determine before 1 time, and as ordain 1 time; for the 6 total.

The first occurance of the word gives clear indication of its meaning: Acts 4:28 "For to do whatsoever thy hand and thy counsel determined before <4309> to be done."   Here, an act is predetermined. The time frame of the determining is not certain in the the word usage; the Augustinian and Reformed theologian is certain that it is always before the foundation of the earth but you and I must not presume, or especially pre-assume such, especially in Acts 4:28.

In our previous discussion we have demonstrated that Paul's use of the word in Romans 8 is clearly in the corporate sense: Rom 8:29 "For whom he did foreknow, he <4309> also did predestinate <4309> *to be* conformed to the image of his Son, that he might be the firstborn among many brethren.
Rom 8:30 Moreover whom he did predestinate <4309>, them he also called: and whom he called, them he also justified: and whom he justified, them he also glorified."

Recall that the theme of Romans chapter 8 is the function of the Holy Spirit in the believer's life with an emphasis on assuring that you are truly indwelt by Christ. This can be seen by highlighting the occurrences of the word 'if' in verses 9-13 . Verses 14-17 go on to establish how one knows if they are 'in Christ' and verses 18-25 deals with the believers *"earnest expectation"* and hope. Verses 26-28 addresses our infirmities and dealings with *"all things"* and in verses 29 and 30 we find Paul reckoning that God will certainly take care of his own. Notice that this care, foreknowledge, predestination, calling, justification, and glorification is towards God's people corporately in this context. Notice also that calling is to service as previously established, and the justification and glorification are in the perfect tense indicating the ongoing aspect of their working.

Thus in Romans 8 the predestination is not towards an individual pre-destined to salvation or justification, but is unequivocally in the corporate sense, i.e. That the body of believers, found in the body of Christ, are foreknown corporately, are predestined corporately, are called to service corporately, are being justified corporately and are being glorified corporately. Rom 8:29-30 is none other than a corporate predestination of the saints and is never, never to be construed as individual unsaved souls predestined for salvation!

Look now at the 4th use of word# 4309, προορίζω : 1Co 2:7 "But we speak the wisdom of God in a mystery, *even* the hidden *wisdom*, which God ordained <4309> before the world unto our glory:"

Notice here what was predestined before the world, ... it is "the hidden wisdom." In other words it was pre-ordered that man would have only part of the wisdom of God revealed in a progressive revelation. Thus, mystery would be revealed, and some mystery will remain. It will remain until we see him face to face. Now, "looking through a glass darkly"(1Cor 13:12), our perfect understanding of things of an infinite God are darkened by our finite mind and His finite revelation. That is awesome when you consider that we will have finite minds contemplating an infinite God for an eternity.

The last two uses of word# 4309, προορίζω are found in Paul's letter to Ephesus: Eph 1:5 "Having predestinated <4309> us unto the adoption of children by Jesus Christ to himself, according to the good pleasure of his will, Eph 1:11 In whom also we have obtained an inheritance, being predestinated <4309> according to the purpose of him who worketh all things after the counsel of his own will:"

As stated earlier, Ephesians chapter 1 is a mainstay for the Augustinian and Calvinist errant reasoning. They will continue to look at these verses as individual soul election and individual soul predestination despite the clear context of their corporate usage. This introduction and the clear development of these concepts in the body of this epistle are clearly not addressing anyone but those who are already born again into Christ. The choosing and the predestination found in Ephesians chapter one, follow the choosing, election and predestination of saints throughout the Bible as the corporate 'in Christ' and not as individual choosing of lost souls for salvation. One becomes elect by being 'in Christ.' Those 'in Christ' are predestined for certain things. And one can get 'in Christ' only be a volitional act of their will to believe, confess, and call on the Lord Jesus Christ. Once one has done so they are predestined unchangeably. If one has not done so, their fate is not predetermined but rests on their decision to accept the only begotten Son of God. To not accept, they remain condemned before God. "For God sent not his Son into the world to condemn the world: but that the world through him might be saved. He that believeth in him is not condemned, but he that believeth not is condemned already, because he hath not believed in the name of the only begotten son of God." (John 3:17-18) Become a believer and you become predestined.

Chapter 9 Election and the Sovereignty of God

The Bible teaches that God has sovereignty and this sovereignty speaks of God's supreme, permanent authority in the universe, in this world and in nations of this world. Man, created in God's image, however, is given the self governing authority to freely make moral, ethical and operational decisions for himself.   Attributing the decisions of man to the sovereignty of God trivializes his permanent and supreme authority and removes man's responsibility for his own decisions. God, in His sovereignty has created man with a free will and although He knows the heart of man in general, He ponders the heart of man (Prov 5:21, 21:2, 24:12) and allows mans free choice. Although He knows the direction of man in general, He places choices before man and reacts in real time to the direction man chooses. Although He knows mans natural course of rebellion, He intervenes divinely to accomplish His purposes. Although this divine intervention can change an individuals course, and/or the course of a nation, God's intervention will work His divine ends and God's intervention is always intended to turn man from sin and toward righteousness, without violating mans free will and self governing choice.

In this chapter we shall briefly examine the sovereignty of God, and only partially separate that from God's omniscience which will be examined in greater detail in the next chapter where we examine God's foreknowledge. By sovereignty we mean that God exercises supreme permanent authority and control over all things. By 'supreme' we mean that there is none higher. By permanent we mean that he has always been and will always be sovereign. By authority and control we mean that God alone authorizes every action and no actions occur without his authorization and that he is in control of every action (and every circumstance surrounding an action) and that no action occurs but what He is in complete control. By all things we mean all his created things, to include the breath of the righteous and the wicked; the burning hydrogen of our sun and every star (if indeed the scientific theories about the sun and stars prove true, recall that theories do not become truth or law until proven experimentally no matter how many 'scientists' accept a theory as factual) as well as the burnt carbohydrates producing every finger movement, and every ant, coney, locust and spider. He authorizes and is in control of the electrons orbiting every cluster of protons and neutrons, (if there truly are such particles as we theorize,) and the forces of gravity, electro magnetics and nuclear energy by which all things consist. Such infinite authority and control is too wonderful for us of finite mind, and such is the sovereignty of the infinite Jehovah God.

Now, with such an unfathomable infinite sovereignty in view, we must state that God created man in his image and after his fashion, to have a free decision making, path choosing, volitional will. In order for it to remain free and volitional it must remain outside of the direct control of an otherwise sovereign God. Although God controls every impulse my brain sends down my spine to secure my next heart beat, the thoughts and intents of my 'heart' are given free rein. My, thoughts and intents are surely known by God but in the Bible, that is always in real time, not in future time. If you doubt this, the word 'thought(s)' occurs 134 times in the Bible, in an hour or two you can examine every occurrence for yourself. You will find them to be present tense in relation to Gods thinking and working toward man; it is always in real time, with man's thought and direction free from God's foreknowledge or control and man's thoughts pondered by God in real time. This is an awesome truth that will need repeating when we examine God's foreknowledge. It is also a challenging truth for one grounded in Augustinian theology, I encourage such a one to finish this book taking note of its outline and argument, and then prayerfully read His book, Genesis to Revelation and see if this truth rings true to Scripture. Remember Dr. Clifford on Praed Street and spend more time with Scripture than you do with other influences and you will find the real time relationship with Him more precious every pass through His book. After a couple passes through all of Scripture, find this book again and you will find yourself in full agreement on this truth.

In faulty theology God can reel time backward and forward like I do a movie reel full of fixed unchangeable pictures and sounds. That is ground breaking, perfectly logical, quite understandable, somehow appealing theology but it is NOT true nor implied in any Biblical revelation. Therein God operates in *real* time not in *reel* time. For this chapter on sovereignty understand that man is given a mobility of thought and action which are outside of God's sovereignty, i.e. God in sovereignty allows man a mobility outside of His direct control. This is an awesome reckoning which directly violates Augustinian, Reformed and Calvinistic theology. If you get a grasp of this truth from Scripture I hardly need to continue in the theme of Biblical election and foreknowledge. Getting a hold of this concept, and unhinged from the restricting 'infinite divine plan' concept of Calvinism, will open all the Scriptures to a new light that puts election, predestination and foreknowledge in their proper corporate perspective.

Perhaps here, we should all examine the 134 referenced verses to better understand God's thoughts and mans thoughts, germane and key to this discourse. It could shake loose the 'infinite divine plan' misnomer ingrained by 1,700 years of erroneous teaching and give new insight about what God does and does not foreknow about my grand children's salvation. Baptists, of all people, need to get their faith and practice on this subject from the Bible and not from the theology books of old.

It is then crucial that one understands this last statement. Understanding this concept of mans volitional will frees me from the error of Calvinistic theology that is rooted in Augustinian misconception about free will. For man to maintain his position as a free moral agent, God can not impose a direct control of his will. We shall see this in Scripture as we examine God's use of in-direct control of nature and all creation to bring about his will and purposes in mankind. When God is in direct charge of every part of his creation except the will of man, we find him well able to direct mans ways when that is his desire and purpose.

In Deut 7:20 and Joshua 24:12 we find an excellent example of God making people willing to leave his promised land without use of the sword of his chosen people Israel. He did not use mind control on the Amorites, He simply controlled the hornets in the land and the Amorites made a free volitional decision to vacate the premise. I have done the same on several occasions back on the farm. Hornets can be very persuasive. God can be more so.

Calvinism characteristically carries with it the fatalistic view that God's sovereignty makes men nothing more than pieces on an eternal chess board where God is playing a game, and we are but pawns in the sovereigns hand. No, not so, indeed God can not make man do one thing or the other, go one way or another, even think one thought or the other, or else he will violate the free volitional will that

he has placed in man in making him a free moral agent.
Understanding this makes us cognizant that God did not, and can not
create or cause evil, rebellion or sin. He made man a free moral agent,
placed him in a garden with that freedom, wherein the opposer of God
persuaded man towards a decision. That decision plunged man into
death and a sin nature. God did not cause that decision but he
authorized it, he allowed it of his free moral agents, yeah He even
accommodated it and before the foundation of the earth he had a plan
to redeem that race of man, fallen into sin.

When one wants modeling clay to be hardened they would
withhold water from it and allow time and sunshine to dry it out some.
You would say that they hardened the modeling clay. They didn't.
They withheld the water from it and it hardened as was its nature.
Consider again that for man to maintain his free moral will, God can
not directly impose upon that volitional will. Now consider that in
Exod, 4:21, 7:3,13,14,22, 8:19, 9:7, 12,35, 10:1,20,27, 11:10, 14:4,
14:8 God hardened Pharaoh's heart. (in 8:15,32,and 9:34 Pharaoh
hardened his own heart and some use these references to justify or
somehow rationalize the other 15 heart hardening references. I would
not long rest on such a shallow argument.) God did not use mind
control on Pharaoh, nor pre-orchestrate the DNA or genes to make
Pharaoh think a certain way. God hardened Pharaoh's heart the same
way one hardens clay. He can back off and let nature take its course,
our nature is to harden when left short of grace and mercy. God did
not reach inside of Pharaoh and twist some brain cells to make
Pharaoh's heart hard. He simply backed away his heart softening
presence from him and the nature of Pharaoh took over to harden his
heart. Thus God did harden Pharaoh's heart, as one hardens clay's
heart. Again God can not withdraw the free moral agency given to
any man. But he can withdraw his gracious hand and let them harden
as is their nature.

In continuing with our insistence that God can not directly
impose upon mans volitional will we must examine Judas' betrayal and
Peter's denial. We shall contend that for cases of fulfilled prophecy
God brings special influences to bear in order to secure the result.
(Let's not be so presumptuous as to think that what God did to directly
fulfill his prophecy he must necessarily do for you or I) Such special
influences come to bare on Judas and Peter. But we can still contend
that God did not use mind control or rob Judas nor Peter of their free

volition will. We thus contend that, in his sovereignty, God used his control over all the circumstances involved in Judas' betrayal and Peter's denial, but did not cause either. Again it was the withdrawal of His gracious hand and presence that let Judas do what was in his nature, and allowed Peter to do what was in his nature.

Augustus H. Strong wrote much on the omniscience of God in his book "Systematic Theology." He says of God's perfect, eternal and immediate knowledge that:

> "Since God knows things as they are, he knows the necessary sequences of his creation as necessary, the free acts of his creation as free, the ideally possible as ideally possible. God knows what would have taken place under circumstances not now present:[80]"...

Thus God's perfect, eternal and immediate knowledge of all things to include our very thoughts (Psalm 139:2 "understandeth my thoughts afar off" note that this is afar off in distance and need not be afar off in time!) and God's sovereign control of all things animate or inanimate, make him well equip to bring special influences to bear in order to secure the fulfillment of prophecy concerning Judas' betrayal and Peters denial. These he used without creating or causing the act of man but in authorizing and allowing it to come to pass via mans volitional will.

The emphasis then of this short examination of God's sovereignty is to insist that such sovereignty can not impose on mans free volitional will, and can not author wickedness nor sin. When God created man as a free moral agent he voluntarily surrendered some sovereignty in that he does not have direct control over the mind of man but exercises indirect control to fulfill his prophecies and accomplish his purposes.

In that God can not author wickedness the following anonymous story illustrates so well:

Did God Create Everything?

The university professor challenged his students with this question.
Did God create everything that exists?
A student bravely replied "yes, he did!"
"God created everything?" The professor asked.
"Yes, sir," the student replied.
The professor answered, "If God created everything, then God created

---

[80] Strong, Augustus H., "Systematic Theology", page 284

evil since evil exists, and according to the principle that our works define who we are then God is evil."

The student became quiet before such an answer.

The professor was quite pleased with himself and boasted to the students that he had proven once more that Christian faith was a myth.

Another student raised his hand and said, "Can I ask you a question professor?"

"Of course," replied the professor.

The student stood up and asked, "Professor, does cold exist?"

"What kind of a question is this? Of course it exists. Have you never been cold?" The students snickered at the young man's question.

The young man replied, "In fact sir, cold does not exist.

"According to the laws of physics, what we consider cold is in reality the absence of heat. Every body or object is susceptible to study when it has or transmits energy, and heat is what makes a body or matter have or transmit energy. Absolute zero (-460 degrees F) is the total absence of heat; all matter becomes inert and incapable of reaction at that temperature. Cold does not exist. We have created this word to describe how we feel if we have no heat."

The student continued. "Professor, does darkness exist?"

The professor responded, "Of course it does."

The student replied, "Once again you are wrong sir, darkness does not exist either. Darkness is in reality the absence of light. Light we can study, but not darkness. In fact we can use Newton's prism to break white light into many colors and study the various wavelengths of each color. You can not measure darkness. A simple ray of light can break into a world of darkness and illuminate it. How can you know how dark a certain space is? You measure the amount of light present. Isn't this correct?

Darkness is a term used by man to describe what happens when there is no light present."

Finally the young man asked the professor, "Sir, does evil exist?"

Now uncertain, the professor responded, "Of course, as I have already said. We see it every day. It is in the daily example of man's inhumanity to man. It is in the multitude of crime and violence everywhere in the world. These manifestations are nothing else but evil."

To this the student replied, "Evil does not exist sir, or at least it does not exist unto itself. Evil is simply the absence of God. It is just like darkness and cold, a word that man has created to describe the absence of God. God did not create evil. Evil is not like faith, or love that exist just as does light and heat. Evil is the result of what happens when man does not have God's love present in his heart. It's like the cold that comes when there is no heat or the darkness that comes when there is no light."

The professor sat down. The young man's name is ... unknown.
Anonymous

(Note: It was reported on the internet that the student was Albert Einstein, but such a source has lost credibility Such an account is found nowhere in Albert's writings, if it was credited to him by a witness that witness remains unavailable for comment. It was likely not the Jewish Genius, Albert Einstein, it is likely a fictitious accounting, but it is genius just the same.)

Chapter 10 Election and God's Foreknowledge

God's foreknowledge must necessarily be examined with some careful consideration of definitions. Theologians of the past have intermingled God's foreknowledge with His omniscience and His sovereignty to where, in their mind, all three must be be infinite and interconnected. If God, who knows everything, foreknows an event will happen, then it surely shall and it is thus fixed and unchangeable. If an event is fixed and unchangeable then someone must have decreed it be so and the only one that could so decree is the sovereign God. Thus, in their mind, an infinite omniscience makes infinite foreknowledge brought about by supreme sovereignty. This is very logical and very simple, but not very Scriptural. In this examination God's foreknowledge, omniscience and sovereignty must be untangled from each other. Such examination will necessarily put some strain on ones pre-defined attributes of omniscience and sovereignty, and thus make one the target of serious accusations of heresy. The unifying of ones theology with Scripture is still well worth the mental strain and the accusers daggers.

The Bible teaches God's foreknowledge whereby God foreordained some events for certain before the foundation of the earth. Because there are only five foreknown events specifically called out by Scripture; and because fixing all future events with certain foreknowledge makes them fixed and fatalistic; and because locking all events into providence or fate robs man of his free moral agency; one must contend that there are events and things in the future that are not decreed by God and are thus not foreordained, not predestined, and thus remain outside of God's foreknowledge.

Man's ability to choose his destiny in eternity, his course in life, his course in any one day and his minutest decision or action, is not, and can not with Scripture be locked into a fatalistic fixed model of any sort. Again, there are only 5 (five) major events called out as certain and foreknown by God. God's Word indicates the five were indeed certain, and the prophecy that He gives surrounding these certain/fixed events are certain and brought to pass by God's divine control. The table below calls out these 5 foreknown events which will be expounded later in this chapter:

	Foreknown Event	Scripture that Calls it out
1	That Christ, the only begotten Son of God, would be sent into the world to redeem man.	1Pet 1:20 "Who verily was foreordained <4267> before the foundation of the world, but was manifest in these last times for you,"
2	That His chosen people, Israel would be used in His plan.	Rom 11:2 "God hath not cast away his people which he foreknew <4267>. Wot ye not what the scripture saith of Elias? how he maketh intercession to God against Israel, saying,. "
3	That His Son would be crucified and slain by the wicked hands of man	Acts 2:23 "Him, being delivered by the determinate counsel and foreknowledge <4268> of God, ye have taken, and by wicked hands have crucified and slain:" Acts 4:26-28 "determined before to be done"
4	That '*them that love God*' would through '*all things*', be '*conformed to the image of His son.*'	Rom 8:28 "And we know that all things work together for good to them that love God, to them who are the called according to *his* purpose. 29 For whom he did foreknow <4267>, he also did predestinate *to be* conformed to the image of his Son, that he might be the firstborn among many brethren. 30 Moreover whom he did predestinate, them he also called: and whom he called, them he also justified: and whom he justified, them he also glorified."
5	That corporately believers would be the elect for service '*through the sanctification of the Spirit*'	1Pet 1:2 "Elect according to the foreknowledge <4268> of God the Father, through sanctification of the Spirit, unto obedience and sprinkling of the blood of Jesus Christ: Grace unto you, and peace, be multiplied."

God's Word indicates clearly that man has the free agency to determine his own 'fate'. Man can determine his own daily 'fate' and his own eternal 'fate' and they, then can not be fate, can not be decreed, and cannot then be foreordained or foreknown! The fatalistic idea that God foreknows/foreordains every detail of our life, our death and our eternity springs from Augustinian, Catholic, Reformed and Calvinistic theology and not from Scripture. Scripture ALWAYS shows God working with individuals in a present tense with ample opportunity for changing their future, and NEVER with a fatalistic, foreordained unchangeable future. Thus, God's sovereignty and God's foreknowledge can not by decree nor by causative action, infringe on mans free will to choose. God, instead, works in the heart of every man to lead him to righteousness and God works in all of his creation to accomplish what he has foreordained/ foreknown or prophecied.

From the Bible one can be certain that their destiny, and their neighbor's destiny may be changed by actions, by choices and by prayers on any given day. Reformed theology holds that every thing which is foreknown must come to pass, and if it must come to pass it must be decreed by God, and if it is decreed by God it was decreed before the foundation of the earth. One lends credence to their error when they teach that every breath taken, and every word herein writen was foreknown by God befour the foundation of the world, to include the misspelling of 'before!' This was plainly taught in Dr. Jordan's Calvary <u>Baptist</u> Theological Seminary's systematic theology classes that boasted themselves non-Calvinistic and pro King James. (Both boasts proved hollow.)   What drives the reformed theologian into this certainty of every minuscule event in our future is their misrepresentation of the doctrine of election and the necessity that God must decree who gets in (Calvinism) or must at least foreknow who gets in (Augustinianism and Arminianism) and thereby he must be in control of every infinite detail of our existence (their interpretation of sovereignty). Such an extension of man's logic is not supported in Scripture. Any Bible student can see the importance of breaking the bond of this error. Where we break it will be the source of great discourse and likely some contention. The table below shows the various views that one can take as far as what is contained in God's foreknowledge.

Minimum Biblical	1st Logical Extension	2nd Logical Extension	3rd Logical Extension	Eletist Extention	Calvinistic & Extreme
God foreknows only the 5 specifics called out in scripture and only two of them were specifically stated as foreknown before the foundation of the world. As time, circumstances and man's choices progress God augments his plans.	God foreknows only the 5 specifics called out in Scripture and foreknew them before the foundation of the world. Other events, including prophesied ones are derived and augmented as time, circumstances and mans choices progresses.	God foreknows before the foundation of the world the 5 specifics called out in Scripture, and the prophesied events that he would use to bring them to pass. Other events are derived as time, circumstances, and mans decisions progress.	God foreknows before the foundation of the world every event that he prophesied to come to pass. His planing was complete and sealed before the world began.	God foreknows before the foundation of the world every event in the major players lives (prophets, forefathers, apostles, the Spurgeons n Whitfields etc.) He foreknows and decrees the major events to bring to pass his will and some of us , like Saul/Paul, were elect for salvation.	God foreknows before the foundation of the world every detail of every humans existence; every daily hair count, decision, error and act that every human would do, as well as their salvation decision is foreknown and decreed by God in his infinite plan.

To construe from a study of God's omniscience, sovereignty, and foreknowledge that God has plotted out every detail of one's life is sheer folly that is not supported by Scripture. Augustus H. Strong contrasts his own folly here with this footnote:

> "Aristotle maintained that there is no certain knowledge of contingent future events. Sceinus, in like manner, while he admitted that God knows all things that are knowable, abridged the objects of the divine knowledge by withdrawing from the number those objects whose future existence he considered as uncertain, such as the determinations of free agents. These, he held, can not be certainly foreknown, because there is nothing in the present condition of things from which they will necessarily follow by natural law. The man who makes a clock can tell when it will strike. But free-will, not being subject to mechanical laws, can not have its acts predicted or foreknown. Milton seems also to deny God's foreknowledge of free acts: "So, without least impulse or shadow of fate, Or aught by me immutable foreseen, they trespass."[81]

We shall examine some Scripture that fully illustrates the true concept of foreknowledge and detracts from a notion that God foreknows and has predetermined the events in individual lives. But a vivid and present illustration of it can be found in Mt 10:30 "But the very hairs of your head are all numbered." In this verse God is revealing how

---

[81] Strong, Augustus H., *"Systematic Theology"* pp 284

valuable we are to him and revealing an infinite omniscience. It is pointed out that this is present tense omniscience. One can not imply from this verse that God knows how many hairs they will have in their head tomorrow. In fact if they grab a handful right now and enter into a silent debate about weather to tug on them or not, Aristotle and Sceinus ventured that God does not know which choice they would make, it is their free will as a free agent to pull them out, and God does not know how many hairs they will have in the next seconds; it is not knowable because God has made us free moral agents. If one did pull, God knows exactly how many were pulled and how many they have left in their head. This is present tense omniscience. All of the Scriptures used to support God's omniscience are present tense circumstances and do not infringe on mans free agency to choose. The theologian argues with his logic that God must have known before hand whether one would pull them out or not, but Scripture does not support such supposition. Such a supposition dashes against man being a free moral agent, and it is hypothesized without supporting Scripture. God's omniscience is always rendered in the present tense, not extended to future acts except where it touches his only begotten Son and the five things that He clearly foreknew and foreordained. Lets examine the Scriptures.

Examine with me how the Bible uses the word "foreknow." J. Strong's word #4267, προγινοσκω [82] shows up only 5 times in Scripture, and its noun 'foreknowledge', is used only twice. First note J. J. Strong's entry for the word:

Foreknow

4267 προγινοσκω proginosko *prog-in-oce'-ko* from 4253 and 1097; verb

Translated as foreknow 2 times (Rom 8:29,11:12), as foreordain 1 time (1Pet 1:20), as know 1 time (Acts 26:5), as 'know before' 1 time (2Pet 3:17); for the 5 times it occurs in the Bible.

Of course to foreknow by definition is simply know beforehand. We again avoid Strong's definition here because of his

---

[82] There is a reluctance by some to use the Greek in their studies because we have a supreme English translation in the KJV. The author holds tenaciously to the latter but finds word studies of Greek roots is most effectively done in the Greek or with the Strong's numbering system.

bent toward the error of Calvinism and we have already demonstrated that there are none "elected to salvation" ... only "elected to service." But please take note of the synonymous use of 'foreknow' and 'foreordain' giving credence to the fact that in Scripture God does not foreknow something without being the causative agent that fore-ordains or decrees that it comes to pass. Thus in this treatise, as in the theology books, 'to foreknow' is 'to foreordain' and 'to foreordain' is 'to decree'. This is true in Scripture, but reformed theologians sometimes try to differentiate the three because of their infinitesimal decreeing /foreknowing/foreordaining. Baptists also try to separate foreknowledge from foreordaining and decrees. A decree is causative, i.e. not that God just allowed for something but that God planned it, yea, he decreed that it would come to pass. This important syntax *mine field* must be properly negotiated. If God foreknows something, it is fixed and will come to pass. Ones free will actions, choices, and decisions can not change it. Then it must be fixed by someone and thus decreed. If the infinitesimal is foreknown, it is likewise foreordained, decreed, and planned, and this planning can only be done by an infinite one who decrees. Herein we contend that the infinitesimal can not be foreknown else all free will is lost.

With these definitions in place examine the noun for the usage of:

Foreknowledge

4268 προγνωσις prognosis *prog'-no-sis* from 4267; noun.

Translated as foreknowledge 2 times in the Bible. Again in definition foreknowledge is often tied to pre-arrangement and should be examined with another word **Predestinate** 4309 προοριζω proorizo *pro-or-id'-zo* verb, Translated in the AV-predestinate 4 times (Rom 8:29,30, Eph 1:5,11), determine before 1 time (Acts 4:28), and ordain 1 time (1Cor 2:7); for the 6 times in the New Testament. The ladder is treated elsewhere in this treatise. We examine only Acts 4:28 under our consideration of God's foreknowledge.

Before examining the five things called out in God's foreknowledge lets look at how the word is used for man's foreknowledge. First in: Acts 26:5 "Which knew <4267> me from the beginning, if they would testify, that after the most straitest sect of our religion I lived a Pharisee." Notice in this context that the word is used of a foreknowledge that the Jews had of Paul's manner of life from (his) youth. This foreknowledge was human and looks back on what was known, and not ahead with any knowledge of the future. This is an important aspect of God's foreknowledge as well.

The second use of the word in this sense is: 2Pe 3:17 "Ye therefore, beloved, seeing ye know these things before <4267>, beware lest ye also, being led away with the error of the wicked, fall from your own steadfastness." Again here is the use of the word to show something that is known before, not in predicting the future, or knowing before time, but in knowing before in time. In these instances, notice that pre-arrangement or foreordaining is not connected with its usage. Let's now examine the 5 things that God foreknew, and foreordained, and possibly decreed that they would come to pass. (In the Bible man writes decrees not God, theologians like this word, 'decree', applied to God's directing of things, Scripture does not.)

The Bible tells us that God foreknows, foreordains, or pre-decrees 5 major events as specifically called out in Scripture. **First**, it was foreordained before the foundation of the world, that Christ, the only begotten Son of God, would be sent into the world to redeem man. (1Pet 1:20 "Who verily was foreordained <4267> before the foundation of the world, but was manifest in these last times for you,") Again be careful separating what is foreknown from what is foreordained. The two spring from the same Greek word and must logically coincide but an abstraction often accompanies our understanding of their difference. Here, it should be said that many many events are prophesied about this foreordained event. These prophecies reveal details about how God will bring to pass what he has foreordained. These individual prophecies are never refered to as 'foreordained' or 'foreknown' in the Scriptures. If the Scriptures do not confuse the foreordained with the prophesied detail we should not either. All the major theologians intertwine the foreordained with the prophesied, with the inner workings of God. In reality the foreknown / foreordained event and the detailed prophesied events that bring them to pass and the inner workings of God do not intertwine but remain separable in concept.

Theologians use the three strand cord of foreknowledge/ foreordaining/ decrees to rope in an errant theology stating that God 'foreknows' how ones day will go tomorrow, what decisions they will make, and the number of hairs they may or may not end up with next year. They will declare that God 'foreknows' whether ones aunt, father, or child will get saved or will not get saved and that such an event is cast in stone and unalterable in God's plan. They will say that God knows the last person to get saved before the return of the Lord Jesus Christ, and that he can not return until that last one gets 'in'. They will say all kinds of these things were predetermined, yeah even predestined before the foundation of the world.   The Bible provides no evidence of this kind of wild speculation. It says in 1Pet 1:20 that Christ's first coming was foreordained before the foundation of the world, nothing more.

Secondly, God 'foreknew' that his people, Israel would be used in his plan. Rom 11:2 "God hath not cast away his people which he foreknew <4267>. Wot ye not what the scripture saith of Elias? how he maketh intercession to God against Israel,... "   God's use of the chosen nation Israel, and the seed of Abraham, was specifically foreknown by God. This was not however, called out to be foreknown before the foundation of the world. Again the theologian presumes via their logic that anything that is foreknown by an infinitely omniscient God, must have been foreknown from the foundation of the world, but such is a step in man's logic and not a revelation of the Holy Scriptures. We shall not utterly deny this eternal foreknowledge of the existence and use of a nation called Israel, but we can not completely support it with Scripture.   In Scripture the use of the nation of Israel is called out to be in God's foreknowledge, but not specifically called out as being in God's plan in existence before the foundation of the world. His plans can be dynamic in time.

Thirdly, the Bible specifically states that God's foreknowledge included the fact that his Son would be crucified and slain by the wicked hands of man.   Acts 2:23 "Him, being delivered by the determinate counsel and foreknowledge <4268> of God, ye have taken, and by wicked hands have crucified and slain:" Acts 4:26-28 also declares that this deed was "determined before to be done" using the Greek word 4309 προορίζω proorizo *pro-or-id'-zo*, verb, to predetermine. Herein one can see that foreknowledge and foreordaining and decreeing of God are directly connected in this context.   An additional revelation about this event is that it was also wrapped in the 'determinate counsel' of God.   Thus the crucification was worked into history by a determination and purpose of God. Just because this was so for the crucifixion, 'the determinate counsel of God' does not necessarily apply to all other foreknown events, and it should especially not be applied to one running out of gas on I-190 in downtown Chicago at 11:30 PM! Running out of gas involves more of ones free will decisions, neglect and stupidity, and no determinate counsel or foreknowledge of God. This does not imply that God did not know they would run out, but that going with the theologian and saying it was decreed before the foundation of the world, trivializes God, trivializes God's plan, and trivializes those things that are specifically revealed to be in his foreknowledge and determinate counsel. At least one's wife knew them enough to *foreknow* that this would happen, and they kept a gallon of gas in their trunk.

Fourth, God said of '*them that love God*', that he '*foreknew*' them, and had predestined that, through '*all things*', they would be '*conformed to the image of His son.*' More exactly he said: Rom 8:28 "And we know that all things work together for good to them that love God, to them who are the called according to *his* purpose. 29 For whom he did foreknow <4267>, he also did predestinate *to be* conformed to the image of his Son, that he might be the firstborn among many brethren. 30 Moreover whom he did predestinate, them he also called: and whom he called, them he also justified: and whom he justified, them he also glorified."

This Scripture does not state that God foreknew the individuals who would choose to '*love God*' and thus come 'into Christ' (vrs 8:1) but that He foreknew that those that '*love God*', and are '*called according to his purpose*', i.e. those 'in Christ' would be '*conformed to the image of his Son*', that would be his brethren. This is an important distinction, and is a reoccurring theme of this thesis. The coming to salvation is not the theme of Romans 8. The theme is what becomes of us, once we are born-again, i.e. converted, justified, quickened, indwelt, and baptized into the body of Christ. Once this has occurred we are predestined. Prior to its occurrence we are given a call, yes, but it is a call to repentance, a call that says "Whosoever shall call upon the name of the Lord shall be saved." If we accept that calling, God saves us and we become, at that point, predestined to be conformed to the image of his Son. Here, he foreknew that he would be the first born among many brethren. Be careful not to mix up the callings here. Be careful that one does not, with these Scriptures, come up with the Calvinistic theology that they, their child or mom were individually chosen for salvation, nor that God's foreknowledge holds a fatalistic assurance that oneself or ones kin will or will not be saved. No such doctrine is found in Romans, particularly not in Romans chapter 8. Additional discussion of Paul's context here is found in Chapter 13 of this work.

In Romans 8 the destiny of those who volitionally got into Christ by the new birth is determined, yea predestined, only '*if so be that the Spirit of God dwell in you.*' (verse 8) Thus, since God, knew them before (i.e. they previously got saved, as 'foreknowledge' is used in other Scriptures) we can understand that their destiny is now determined, (i.e. Predetermined) their calling is now secure, (i.e. they have become the elect), their justification is daily available (i.e. the Greek Aorist[83] tense making it a started process that is ongoing) and their glorification is as certain as their justification (i.e. all of these past tense verbs are actually and equally Aorist tense making each a past tense started, present tense ongoing and future tense certain verb, such a tense has no English equivalent and is thus transliterated from the Greek word as the 'Aorist' tense.) As a believer, there is a place prepared in God's foreordained plan, such a place is very certain. That plan is not individualistic but is for all the believers who are truly indwelt by God (verse 8). It is simply where the believers will end up and God knew it beforehand, their salvation was not foreknown but the final destiny of the saved was foreknown. If, in the past, one was saved by the Blood of Jesus Christ then God foreknows their predestination in this sense. There is no reason that such a sentence carries back to the foundation of the earth. It does not. Even as Acts 26:5 and 2 Peter 3:17 do not carry back to the foundation of the world, Rom 8:29 does not. Again we must emphasize, whether or not one will end up as a believer is not foreordained by God but left as a 'whosoever will' decision of man.

The **fifth and last** event specifically called out in the New Testament as belonging in God's foreknowledge is that of a corporate

---

[83] Aorits Tense, Most commonly the Aorist tense makes each verb a past tense started, present tense ongoing and future tense certain verb, such a tense has no English equivalent and is thus transliterated from Greek word as the 'Aorist' tense. Aoristos meaning indefinite, or from horizon to horizon. Strongs Note: The aorist tense is characterized by its emphasis on punctiliar action; that is, the concept of the verb is considered without regard for past, present, or future time. There is no direct or clear English equivalent for this tense, though it is generally rendered as a simple past tense in most translations. The events described by the aorist tense are classified into a number of categories by grammarians. The most common of these include a view of the action as having begun from a certain point ("inceptive aorist"), or having ended at a certain point (" cumulative aorist"), or merely existing at a certain point (" punctiliar aorist"). The categorization of other cases can be found in Greek reference grammars.

group of believers who were now elect for service. These people, that by their free will became believers in answer to the call "whosoever will," would be the elect for service '*through the sanctification of the Spirit*' just as Israel was elect for her service through the sanctification of the law. It is recorded as: 1Pet 1:2 "Elect according to the foreknowledge <4268> of God the Father, through sanctification of the Spirit, unto obedience and sprinkling of the blood of Jesus Christ: Grace unto you, and peace, be multiplied." Again this foreknown election is described here as belonging to believers only, and can not be referenced to any unregenerate unbeliever chosen to get into the kingdom of God.   The unsaved never fall into a category of elect or unelect. The decision is always theirs to be made, and every one who has the 'true light' lighten them (John 1:9) can be part of this elect by being part of 'The Elect One', Jesus Christ. All born again believer are elect for obedience and for service. No unbeliever is elect in this sense, but they stand condemned (John 3:16-18) until they become believers. (John 3:36)

Only these five specific events are called out in Scripture as belonging in God's foreknowledge. Only these five can be defended with Scripture as being foreordained. Only these five and no others could ever be called foreknown decrees of God which are called out in the Bible. They are that 1) Christ would come, it was foreknown before the foundation of the world; 2) that Israel would bring the Messiah, it was foreknow in time, not necessarily before the foundation of the world; 3) that Christ would be delivered and crucified, it was in God's determinate counsel and foreknowledge; 4) that regenerate believers are corporately in God's foreknowledge; and lastly 5) that corporately believers would be the elect to serve as His witness' and preachers, it was foreknown in time, not necessarily before the foundation of the world.   From this list of five the theologians begin to add their own list of things that by man's rational thinking 'must have been' a decree of God. These things, they argue, must also have been decreed from the foundation of the earth. These things, they errantly contend, are locked into God's plan from the foundation of the world. That may be logical but it is not Scriptural.

Clearly events locked into the foreknowledge of God, can not be altered by the free will decisions of man. Thus His foreknowledge is in direct contrast to mans free will. God's foreknown events will be brought about and are unavoidable and unalterable. When one tries to make every thing that is, every minute event of ones individual life, something that is locked into fate by the foreknowledge of God, they do err and remove the God given ability to 'choose you this day' the course of ones life.

One thereby looses the responsibility that rests on every choice that determines ones own destiny, ones own consequences. If it is so, that God can reel through time, back and forth, as one would reel an unalterable movie film; if God can know every detail of ones individual existence with the same locked in certainty that one knows the details and the ending of the movie "It's a Wonderful Life." then such events are unalterable by any decision or choice that one could make. God is not so shallow as to reel through unalterable films of our life, numerous Scriptures deny this. Thus, despite the theologians insistence on decrees, foreknowledge and that ones every breath is predetermined and locked in, (to include ones last breath and the very time and place of their taking it) such fatalism can not be supported by Scripture or by logic. Such locked in, destined events of the future are unalterable by any prayer that one could pray; such events can not change even while it is known that God puts two paths before man each day. Thus, despite the teachings of the theologians trained in Calvinistic theology, God did not 'decree' nor hold in his foreknowledge as a foreordained event, that one would on this date do this or that. Thus, one can not hold to the Westminster Confession that *"God did from all eternity, by the most just and holy counsel of his own will, freely and unchangeably ordain whatsoever comes to pass."* It is errant. It does not align with Scripture.

The Bible is replete with evidences that God lays decisions before a man and waits for his choice before determining his next move. Such choices should not be trivialized by fussing with the shallow idea that 'God knew what they would choose and already had his fate assured anyway.' Scripture evidences dictate the freeness of the will of man and preclude the fatalistic foreknowledge of God in the details. The reformed theologian tries to lock each in a 'decree of God', but the Bible never locks such into foreknowledge. Examine some Scriptures that demonstrate a God who is dynamically working out his plan in real time and some that theologians take out of context concerning foreknowledge.

When reading any accounting of God's dealing with man it is obvious that God takes action based on what the man thinks, does, and says. Scripture indicates that God does change his plan and intentions while his attributes never change. Scriptures indicate that God does not foreknow (thus foreordain) individual details, actions and decisions of men, though he knows the heart of man. The theologians which believe otherwise struggle endlessly with Genesis chapter 6 where it "repented the LORD that he had made man on the earth, and it grieved him at his heart." or chapter 11 where "the LORD came down to see the city and the tower which the children of men builded" and therein God made a decision about what 'they' (the trinity of the Godhead, for it says "Let **us** go down and there confound ... ") would do in re-action to this new development. They obviously did not go down to see, so much as to decide.

Reformed theologians have applied two words for these Scriptures that confound their very theory of decrees. The first is to call them an "antinomy" wherein two seeming contradictory laws are both true. The problem with this use is they have no grounds on which to make their 'Law of Decrees' a standing law to begin with. The second word they introduce is 'anthropomorphic' or 'anthropopathic' wherein human motivations, characteristics behavior and feelings are attributed to God so that we can better understand God's essence. Thus, in essence they say, God does not actually have eyes nor ears, though the Bible says he does, God does not 'change his mind' though the Bible says he does, and God does not 'come down to see' though the Bible says he did. These are just written, they say, deceitfully so us mere humans can comprehend an incomprehensible God that the theologians have begun to comprehend for us. Be careful of using antinomy and anthropomorphics in Bible reading, it is far better to read God's word to literally than to consider Scripture deceitful.

The theologians antinomy and anthropomorphic tactic to deny these Scriptures is futile. To contend that God making man in His image and after His likeness carries a lot more weight than their 'anthropomorphicism.' God does not deceive in His word so that man can understand better; he reveals himself in his word so that man can understand perfectly. Actually God reveals himself, and does so without deception or contradiction. Just believe that when the Bible says "*God repented*" (i.e. changed his mind and direction) that '*God repented*' (i.e. changed his mind and direction). It is clear that when God "*came down to see*" for himself, ... that God '*came down to see*' for himself. It is so much more accurate, simple, and reliable to take things literally, as God intends.

Consider that God said "Shall I hide from Abraham that thing which I do; seeing Abraham shall surely become a great and mighty nation, and all the nations of the earth shall be blessed in him?" (Gen 18:17-18) and that He reveals himself as a God who is making a decision about what to tell Abraham because of developing events. He goes on in this self debating decision making process and says :"For I know him, that he will command his children and his household after him, and they shall keep the way of the LORD, to do justice and judgment; that the LORD may bring upon Abraham that which he hath spoken of him." (verse 19) His decision to tell Abraham is based on His knowledge of Abraham in present tense and NOT on any ability of knowing the future in every infinitesimal detail as in one reeling time forward to see. God then closes this chapter with an intimate dialog with Abraham "face to face as a man speaketh unto a friend." (Spoken of Moses and God in Exod 33:11) Was this dialog vain and meaningless to God, intended only to play out a plan of God and manipulate a man named Abraham? Or was God "pondering the heart of man" and speaking "as a friend speaketh unto a friend?" The Bible reveals the latter and contradicts the former time and again.

In the prologue to the poetry written by "a man in the land of Uz, whose name was Job;" we find a contest between God and Satan in its initial framing. This marvelous accounting is hated by modernists and rejected by modern scholars but if it were really inaccurate, be sure that the Lord Jesus Christ, the manifestation of God on Earth, would have been obligated to point out the error instead of insisting that every jot and tittle was profoundly accurate and permanent. In this prologue, presuming the contest was real and genuine as born again Bible believers do, God knew Job and his integrity, not the infinitesimal details that were to unfold in the contest. God knows "the end from the beginning" (Isa 46:10) to be sure, but God does not 'reel the film of time' ahead, check the future then come back and set up a contest with Satan like a schoolboy who cheated on a final exam. God knew Job, yes, tis true, but he watched, and listened, and pondered as the contest unfolded in revealing detail and he responded with a real time input that is most revealing about the God we worship. To say that God foreknew and Sovereignly controlled every detail, every decision, every word of wisdom that would be spoken in Job's record is to trivialize the whole accounting into worthless rubbish. To call it anthropomorphic is ludicrous! No, indeed, this was a genuine contest that took place, and speculating that God '*did from all eternity .. freely and unchangeably ordain whatsoever comes to pass*' (as stated in the Westminster Confession) is but desensitizing us to the reality that God works with us in the present tense and re-acts to the acts, thoughts and prayers that emit from our body, soul and spirit. Reading the epic poem of Job in one sitting will convince any reasonable skeptic that God is making interactive decisions as time goes along, based on the thoughts, actions and integrity of men.

Examine this revealing Scripture in Isa 48:4-7 "Because I knew that thou *art* obstinate, and thy neck *is* an iron sinew, and thy brow brass; 5 I have even from the beginning declared *it* to thee; before it came to pass I shewed *it* thee: lest thou shouldest say, Mine idol hath done them, and my graven image, and my molten image, hath commanded them. 6 Thou hast heard, see all this; and will not ye declare *it*? I have shewed thee new things from this time, even hidden things, and thou didst not know them. 7 They are created now, and not from the beginning; even before the day when thou heardest them not; lest thou shouldest say, Behold, I knew them. "

Clearly here God created some new things to deal with Israel's actions, things that were not from the beginning. The Calvinist doctrine of decrees can not be more clearly denied than it is in this Scripture. God is making up his plans as he goes and deals with ones action or inaction, ones thoughts or decisions in real time and the details are NOT all laid out from the foundation of the world they depend on actions that man takes within his free will. That God foreknows every thing that will happen in the future necessitates fixity, i.e. future events are fixed, they are certain. In Scripture there is very limited fixity and a majority of fluidity i.e. future events are dynamic, they are dependent on mans actions, thoughts, and prayers.

This fluidity is easily demonstrated in four clear dynamic areas. First, God dynamically changes the future based on our prayers. One Bible example being the prayer of Hezekiah in 2Kings 20. As powerful as any other "thus saith the LORD" in Scripture, this one says "Set thy house in order; for thou shalt die and not live." God had determined that Hezekiah's time had come and his death was imminent. In the next verse we find that Hezekiah "prayed unto the LORD." And in the next verse God changed his plan, dynamically changed it based on a prayer, and turned his prophet on his heal to announce the change of plan. (2 Kings 20:4-5)

Now the fatalistic Calvinist reasons that God knew from the foundation of the earth that Hezekiah was going to pray and that God was going to extend Hezekiah's life. But no such nonsense is communicated in the Scripture. God changed what He said He was going to do, and God changed what He was going to do. Yet the Scripture states "hath he said and shall he not do *it*? Or hath he spoken, and shall be not make good?" (Num 23:19) Calvinists take this verse out of its context and make it say God can not change his plan. Baptists then take grains of that theology and errantly say without exception that God can not change what he said he would do. But He did in 2Kings 20! God did change his plan and his word to his prophet. It is fluid not fixed. They will dig out and quote the Scripture that says "every good gift and every perfect gift is from above, and cometh down from the Father of lights, with whom is no variableness, neither shadow of turning." (James 1:17), Psalms 102:25-27 also gives them an indication that God will never change, but clearly here, God changed what he was going to do with Hezekiah because of his prayer. This is easily resolved by reading all these passages in context and realizing that they speak of some specifics and can not be used as a blanket rule to eliminate God's changing his mind in Genesis 6, 2Kings 20 and Jonah 3:9 In the latter the Ninevites said "Who can tell *if* God will turn and repent, and turn away from his fierce anger, that we perish not?" If one is predisposed to the fixity of Calvinism and opposed to His fluidity as portrayed in His dealings with man, they have trouble with the Ninevite question, but any Bible student knows that God did so repent in the next verse! Jonah 3:10 says "And God saw their works, that they turned from their evil way; and God repented of the evil, that he had said that he would do unto them; and he did *it* not."

While examining Hezekiah's prayer in 2Kings lets look at an instance where God dynamically changes the future around based on the zeal of a King. 2Kings 13:18-19 shows that Joash did not have enough zeal in smiting arrows upon the ground. The number of victories Joash was alloted was according to the number of times he smote the ground. He only got three. (2 Kings 13:25) God acted according to the zeal of Joash. God did not warn him that his zeal in smiting the ground would determine God's decision about victories over Syria, but unless the Bible is purposely misleading in this chapter, God dynamically made a decision that altered the future. There is no indication or possibility that these three victories over Syria were predestined, foreordained or foreknown at the foundation of the world, or at the birth of Joash or on the day before Joash met with Elisha in verse 14. No, God developed His plan dynamically based on Joash's zeal at Elisha's death bed. If the accounting of this Scripture is accurate God is making up his plan daily on the basis of the actions of men. We can thereby conclude that only a very few events are sealed in God's foreknowledge and things impacted by mans choices or decision are not foreordained but fluid. So too, one's decision to accept Christ as Saviour and Lord of their life, is their free will decision.

Again, if the Bible is not meant to deceive us, then Exodus 32:9-14 shows a God that can dynamically change His plan around based on intercessions of man. Herein God offers to destroy the seed of Abraham and raise up his great nation from Moses instead. Was this just an idle mind manipulating offer that God was giving to Moses? Could God have abandoned the 12 son's of Israel at this point and made His chosen nation from the seed of Moses or was this a God playing with the mind of Moses? If the Bible's accounting is accurate then God's offer to Moses was genuine and Moses' intercession could impact the dynamic plan of God. We believe the Scriptures do NOT intentionally lead us into error, and they thus show a plan that is dynamically changeable in many areas, even here in an area as holy as the promises already made to the twelve tribes and particularly the lion of the tribe of Judah. God's plans are not fixed they are fluid.

Lastly, it can be easily demonstrated that God dynamically alters his plan based on the actions of man. None so emphatically demonstrates this aspect of God changing His revealed plan than Jonah chapter three that was already referenced. Here the Bible clearly states that "God saw their works, that they turned from their evil way; and God repented of the evil, that he said that he would do unto them; and he did *it* not." (Jonah 3:10) In this instance God's plans are dynamically altered by the prayers, and fasting and repentance of the Ninevites. The very shallow arguments about God foreknowing they would repent and foreknowing that He would alter His direction remains just that, very shallow. Every indication of Scripture is that there are only the five called out events foreknown in God's plan. Not even all of the five were foreknown before the foundation of the world, and God is otherwise dynamically altering ones future based on their thoughts, acts and prayers in every other detail.

Clearly as we read Scripture it emphasizes God's dynamic fluidity in future events of our lives and never a static fixity of what

91

our future holds. But how can the 1000 years of theology toting a God who 'unchangeably ordains whatsoever comes to pass' be so absolutely wrong? Look how they twist Scripture to support their ill gotten theory.

The Error of Foreknowing one's Salvation.

The reformed theologian defines decrees of God as "That external plan by which God has rendered certain all the events of the universe, past, present and future.[84]" They develop this idea from a few verses that say God has a purpose ... if a purpose he must have a plan ... if there is a plan and he is a perfect, infinite, and omniscient God, it must be a perfect, infinite, and omniscient plan, ergo every trivial detail of a life is locked into God's perfect, infinite, omniscient eternal plan,... 'they say.' Included in this lock down of every event of the universe is whether one will or will not receive Christ as their Saviour in their brief time in God's planned out universe. As Augustus goes on to state:

> "While God's total plan with regard to creatures is called predestination, or fore ordination, his purpose so too act that certain will believe and be saved is called election, and his purpose so too act that certain will refuse to believe and be lost is called reprobation.[85]"

Such an ill fated excursion in logic can not be supported in Scripture. 'They' say that the Scripture declares that all things are included in divine decrees and they use in their shallow defense the verses which talk of God's purpose; Isa 14:26-27 "This is the purpose that is purposed upon the whole earth: and this is the hand that is stretched out upon all the nations. 27 For the LORD of hosts hath purposed, and who shall disannul it? and his hand is stretched out, and who shall turn it back?" But any Bible student could look at the context of this and notice this is for the promised destruction of Babylon and the breaking of the Assyrian in Isa 14:24-25. And any Bible student can discern that this is not something that was purposed "before the foundation of the world" but derived by God in real time, based on the faulty free will decisions and actions of a nation of peoples. God, in this text, even uses the Babylonian's faulty decisions and actions (Isa 14:4) to provide us a 'proverb' that personifies Lucifer himself (vr 12-17) and highlights that man is entangled in a battle (ongoing in real time) of the ages, in

---

[84]   Strong , Augustus H., Systematic Theology pp 353
[85]   Ibid

which the people of Babylon must face a consequence of following the wrong influence ... not the decree ... the influence, not the foreknown plan, the consequence of a wrong free will decision. Clearly here in Isa 14:26-27 the purpose deals only with his foreordaining Israel (one of the five foreknown events revealed in the New Testament as foreordained) and the stretched out hand deals with God's real time intervention in the affairs of nations to secure his purpose. To see this one must only read this whole chapter in context. The reformed theologian only reads it in pretext.

'They' use Isa 46:10-11 "Declaring the end from the beginning, and from ancient times *the things* that are not *yet* done, saying, My counsel shall stand, and I will do all my pleasure: 11 Calling a ravenous bird from the east, the man that executeth my counsel from a far country: yea, I have spoken *it*, I will also bring it to pass; I have purposed *it*, I will also do it." But they miss the clear context of this Scripture that God is continuously, in real time, acting on the remnant of Israel to 'carry' them (vr 3-5) into His foreordained purpose to "place salvation in Zion for Israel my glory." (vr 13) This falls directly in line with the only 5 things foreknown and confounds any idea that every detail of the universe is foreknown, especially as it deals with the rebellion and idolatry of Israel, the theme of this text. No, God is working with man in time to bring about His purpose, and God is changing things, directions, and plans in time as they come up. This Scripture demonstrates that God will work directly with man, in real time decision making and action taking, to ensure his foreknown events (there are only 5 revealed in Scripture) come to pass in the end. Thus it declares that despite the free will of man and his bungling of '*my purposes*' "*I will do all my pleasure.*" Notice again the present tense decision making and actions of God. This gives no indication that every detail of the universe is ordered and fatefully falling in place, but that God is working in real time to "*bring it (*the ending) to pass.*" "Declaring the end from the beginning," and "My counsel will stand," in no way justifies that every minute detail of the universe is pre-decreed by God.

'They' say Dan 4:35 supports infinitesimal decreeing. It says: "And all the inhabitants of the earth *are* reputed as nothing: and he doeth according to his will in the army of heaven, and *among* the inhabitants of the earth: and none can stay his hand, or say unto him, What doest thou?" But again this shows the real time working of God to accomplish a limited plan containing certain events, and that he can not be thwarted in what he has purposed to do. Further it declares that the inhabitants of the earth are so minuscule as to not even fall into consideration. That is quite the opposite of the reformed theologian insisting that every decision of man must be decreed into some infinite perfect omniscient plan.

'They' use Eph 1:11 "In whom also we have obtained an inheritance, being predestinated according to the purpose of him who worketh all things after the counsel of his own will:" but this too shows a God working, i.e. deciding, acting and reacting in real time to bring things into the counsel of his will. There is thus no foreknowledge of minute details of any one, much less of the whole universe, in any one of these Scriptures. The reformed theologian is driven to the false supposition in order to bolster his errant Calvinistic theology that the sovereignty of God is what determines whether one gets saved or one gets damned.

Psalms 119:89-91 says "For ever, O LORD, thy word is settled in heaven. 90 Thy faithfulness *is* unto all generations: thou hast established the earth, and it abideth. 91 They continue this day according to thine ordinances: for all *are* thy servants." This speaks of all 'things' that abide by his ordinances and that all 'things' are his servants. But if one would construe the 'things' to include free moral agents then it is obviously recorded, and today visible, that some of his servants are not doing his will, nor following his plan for their lives.

From Zech 6:1 " And I turned, and lifted up mine eyes, and looked, and, behold, there came four chariots out from between two mountains; and the mountains *were* mountains of brass." Augustus Strong (pp355) even tries to imply that the four spirits of the heavens coming out from between two mountains of brass is an implication of "fixed decrees from which proceed God's providential dealings." Augustus knows full well that brass represents God's judgments. If it were mountains of stone he might have slight credence but none with mountains of brass. There are no fixed decrees found in this verse.

The reformed theologian tries to use Scripture to imply that every good act of man is directly decreed by God because in Isa 44:28 it says "That saith of Cyrus, *He is* my shepherd, and shall perform all my pleasure: even saying to Jerusalem, Thou shalt be built; and to the temple, Thy foundation shall be laid." and Eph 2:10 says "For we are his workmanship, created in Christ Jesus unto good works, which God hath before ordained that we should walk in them." Clearly both of these Scriptures touch direct prophecy and areas where God's foreknowledge are only indirectly in view. Thus these Scriptures can not be used to imply that God knew before hand any decision that one may make, or any good one may do.

The reformed theologian tries to use Scripture to imply that every evil act of man was foreknown and thus decreed by God because Gen 50:20 says "But as for you, ye thought evil against me; *but* God meant it unto good, to bring to pass, as *it is* this day, to save much people alive." or 1Kings 12:15, 24 says "Wherefore the king hearkened not unto the people; for the cause was from the LORD, that he might perform his saying, which the LORD spake by Ahijah the Shilonite unto Jeroboam the son of Nebat. .... 24 Thus saith the LORD, Ye shall not go up, nor fight against your brethren the children of Israel: return every man to his house; for this thing is from me. They hearkened therefore to the word of the LORD, and returned to depart, according to the word of the LORD." Again these Scriptures all detail the present tense real time workings of God to bring about what he had foreknown, and it needs not repeated that there are yet only 5 of those events called out in Scripture.

Examination of Acts 4:27-28, Rom 9:17, 1 Pet 2:8, Rev 17:17 show this same misapplication as 'they' build a straw house containing every infinitesimal decision of the wicked and lay it at the feet of God's decreeing. Their errant doctrine of election drives them to such audacious twisting of Scripture. Their logic is somehow attractive to our fallen nature because even Baptists, who should know the Book, so often follow along like a little puppy and errantly say 'God *foreknows* what will happen next Sunday', 'God *foreknows* if Aunt Tilly will be saved', 'God *foreknows* the day I'll die.' Errantly, one says 'God *foreknows* how many would be in Church today', 'God *foreknows* the last person to be saved before the rapture', etc etc ...' Thus one leans into Reformed theology and away from Scripture when they say 'God *foreknows*,... therefore is in control,.. therefore has decreed,' ... No! It is not in the Bible. God is indeed in control of every fiber of our circumstance, but not through foreknowledge.

In Catholic doctrine if one died suddenly without an ability to get to their priest, who, it is supposed, can absolve their mortal sin, or do their indulgence that could, as it is supposed, clean their slate of venial sin before departing this life, they are in an unfortunate eternal mess. Catholics invented purgatory to help the kinfolk do something about the mess while they lined their pockets with their gold. Notice that how and where one died became an important religious concern for people, and it was therefore taught as doctrine that the time and

95

place and circumstance of every individuals death was already predetermined and unalterable. Such an unsupported idea came from such a ludicrous doctrine that one would think the reformed theologians would have discarded it with their revolt against indulgences. Not so. The reformed theologian holds that every detail of ones death and the day of their departure is sealed in a decree from God. Such a doctrine somehow appeals to our nature. "It was just his time to go." they say. Many understand that some people go well before their 'time' because they did things to their body or motor vehicle that only idiots would do. The reformed theologian takes one verse of the Bible, Job 14:5, and try to teach that the time of ones death is certain and chosen. Again, in context any Bible student can see that this Scripture is talking about how little man can do in his short and terminal time here. It is not that his days are numbered and his demise is predetermined, it is that his life is 'bounded' (bounded by 70 years in Psalms 90:10) and departure final (cf Job 14:10) Now read this argument in context and note the shallowness of the reformed theologians argument.

Job 14:4-10 "Who can bring a clean *thing* out of an unclean? not one. 5 Seeing his days *are* determined, the number of his months *are* with thee, thou hast appointed his bounds that he cannot pass; 6 Turn from him, that he may rest, till he shall accomplish, as an hireling, his day. 7 ¶ For there is hope of a tree, if it be cut down, that it will sprout again, and that the tender branch thereof will not cease. 8 Though the root thereof wax old in the earth, and the stock thereof die in the ground; 9 *Yet* through the scent of water it will bud, and bring forth boughs like a plant. 10 But man dieth, and wasteth away: yea, man giveth up the ghost, and where *is* he?"

Baptists even try to help this doctrine along with a Scripture that says 'it is appointed unto man once to die.' (Heb 9:27) If it is appointed, it must be an appointment, and every appointment has a time and place! Shame on us for trying to help the Catholic's along in their misplaced doctrine with such shallow reasoning. This is not the intent of either of these Scriptures, nor should it be so construed.

There will be those too, who insist that since Jesus knew the intimate details of the Apostle John's death in John 21:22 that he therefore must know every detail of every individuals life and death. Again, in context it is obvious that John 21:22 has no such reference to God decreeing even the time of John's death, not to mention that every individual is not specially chosen and ordained as this beloved and longest living apostle was. The Bible never indicated that the individual events of every individual life or every individual death is dictated in any decree of God. Such an ideology only comes from the erroneous need to dictate how God elects some to salvation and God elects some to damnation. The whole necessity of God making certain every act of man (Calvinism) or of God foreknowing and thus fore planning for every act of man (Arminianism) is completely removed with a proper Biblical understanding of the doctrine of election.

The fallacy in this teaching about decrees, fore ordination and foreknowledge, however, can be most readily seen in this line of thinking. If the date, time and circumstance of death is locked with certainty in the foreknowledge of God, then there is nothing that one can do to change it. If they take steps one way or another to change it, theologians contend that an infinite God "foreknew" what they were going to do so, and nothing really changed. God, they say, can see and foreknow every detail of the future and every molecule involved in ones death. They spend volumes of ink to try and prove that such teaching about foreknowledge (found nowhere in the revelation of God) does not infringe on the free-will or the free moral agency of man. They try to differentiate between mans 'potential' to be 'self determining' and his actually 'becoming' 'self determining' all while locked in the decrees of God. They readily admit that this abstract teaching about God's controlling of our life has adverse effects on mans actions. Augustus sites this example:

> "The farmer, who, after hearing a sermon on God's decrees, took the break-neck road instead of the safe one to his home and broke his wagon in consequence, concluded before the end of his journey that he at any rate had been predestined to be a fool, and that he had made his calling and election sure."[86]

The massive theological struggle with a concept that God must control or foreknow every intimate detail of every individual life fills volumes of theology books and swells the halls of seminaries with debate. Grandiose philosophy and detailed mechanisms have been examined to explain how God controls every event with sovereignty in order to enact his will about who gets 'in' and who gets 'burned'. Whether one sides with the most diluted form of the Calvinist's decrees as described by what B.B. Warfield calls 'congruism' and mystery[87], or if he delves into Arminian foreknowledge methods using

---

[86] Strong, Ibid p 361
[87] Warfield, Benjamin B. "The Plan of Salvation" pp90-91

the intricacy of our DNA (whereby God foreknows via one of the over 30 million combinations of one of the 47 chromosomes of man, the very decision making mechanism that makes him move his finger left or right in any given circumstance[88]!, and such a 'man is a machine' analogy comes from Millard J. Erickson's "Christian Theology," the quagmire of the whole debate springs from their erroneous doctrine of elections. The simple truth is that individuals are not mechanical puppets acting out decrees (Calvinism) or a foreknown movie clip (Arminianism). Individuals can make choices that change their future. Individuals can speak up for Christ and change the eternal destiny of their neighbor. Individuals can pray a prayer and secure from God a change in their circumstance. Individuals can enter a prayer closet and change the direction of a loved one or a nation.

The reformed theologian contends, through endless rhetoric, that man does have a free will, that prayer does change things, and that the Bible does say "whosoever will", all the while he locks man into infinite levels of decrees and foreknowledge which enables him to say God elected some to go to heaven, and some to go to hell. They call their man made conflict between free will and sovereignty a mystery as grand as the unity of God, contrasted with the trinity of God; as grand as gnosticism vs agnosticism; as grand as the humanity of Christ vs his incarnate deity...[89]" etc.   Their conflict of whosoever and election however, is entirely man made. The Bible never states, principles, nor intimidates that every individual decision nor act of man is accounted for in a foreknown plan of God. The whole debate, as congealed as it is, stems from Augustine's and Calvin's misconstrued theory about election of saints.   There is no Biblical evidence that the eternal decision of a man is certain in one direction or another. The extension of this certainty to include every finger movement of a man in some infinite divine plan defies all logic of a rational free moral agent. And it defies the clear Biblical truth that prayer, talking to God, changes things.

A proper understanding of the doctrine of election frees us from this ludicrously and causes us to be the life changing witness' and prayer warriors that God intends us to be. 'They' continue to argue otherwise, but it is obvious that what one believes forms a basis for what one does.   When one believes that God already knows or has

---

[88]   Erickson, Millard J., "Christian Theology" pp 358
[89]   Allen, "Religious Progress" pp110

determined who will get saved and who will not get saved, it will effect their witness, their pursuit of souls and their prayer for souls. When one believes that every detail of every life is laid out in a divine plan and is certain forever, they will not be a prayer warrior that changes the course of souls or nations. Don't believe it. It is herein implored that one get a Biblical understanding of the doctrine of election and thereby forgo the foreboding idea that souls are already predestined or that their destiny is foreknown. When in actuality what they pray, and what they say can make all the difference in the world.

In Scripture foreknowledge and fore ordination of God are synonymous and only pertain to 5 events. In the Bible God's omniscience is always in the present tense and the Alpha and Omega never steps out of the present tense to work his will. He also never steps on the free will of man to work his will. His will is that *"whosoever will may come."* You have His word on it. "It is done. I am Alpha and Omega, the beginning and the end. I will give unto him that is athirst of the fountain of the water of life freely." (Rev 21:6)

In conclusion of this needed analysis on foreknowledge it is obvious that we need to take a re-read of the Bible with an eye open to the fact that God is making interactive decisions as life goes along. God changes his plan in accord to man's freewill decisions. Reading Scripture with this insight can change our daily walk and witness for Christ. The things that happen are not set in a granite of foreknowledge, but depend on ones thoughts, ones prayers, and ones actions. This is obvious in Scripture. It is thus conclude that:

1) The things yet to happen in life are not sealed nor firmed up in fate nor in foreknowledge, not even ones "appointed time" to die is appointed by date, hour, and place.

2) God is dynamically making interactive decisions along the way, as one acts he reacts to change their world. He is not less infinite because of this, He is more infinite; Not less omniscient because of this, He is more omniscient; able to control every infinite detail and interaction of 6 billion people at one time and in real time!

3) The eternal fate or destiny of souls is not foreknown by God it is changeable dependent on mans actions, man's witness, man's prayers.

4) God's actions in ones world and in ones circumstances, are based on their reasoning with Him, based on their zeal for Him, based on their prayers to Him, and based on their actions because of Him.

So act on that. Prayer does indeed change things. It can even change the eternal destiny of souls around you.

Chapter 11 Bible Exegesis and Calvinistic Error

When one assembles a system of theology that contradicts a preponderance of Scriptures the system needs to be modified. Much of systematic theology is based on our logical assembly of a knowledge of God. When logic bumps into some verses which contradict our thinking, the tendency is to gloss over these Scriptures with shallow explanations. Human preference is to keep a system of logic in working order and dismiss Scripture, rather than tweak it to conform to the 'non-conforming' verses.   It has also been said that one does not really need systematic theology, just use the Bible as a theology book. In truth we need to resolve principles and revelation into a system of understanding that first conforms to the Scriptures, and then fits our logical understanding. Calvinism brazenly twists Scripture to maintain mans logical persuasion.

Indeed there are often apparent antinomies which require reasonable explanations before they will reasonably fit into finite minds. An antinomy is "A contradiction between principles or conclusions that seem equally necessary and reasonable."   We find Scripture which says 'Nothing is impossible with God.' and we logically conclude that 'God can do anything.' All well and good, but many people at the county fair are stumped with the riddle "Can you name three things that God can not do?" A frequent answer is "God can do anything!" But God can not lie; God can not change; and God can not let you into His heaven without your accepting His only begotten Son. Systems of thinking often need to be expanded or corrected to account for all Scripture principles. Such correction needs to be done with Calvin's errant doctrine of election.

A prevalent need to allow a doctrine's careful explanation of certain Scriptures can be illustrated with our doctrine of baptism, which gave Baptists their title. Believers who held staunchly to Scripture, baptizing only believers, when compromising churches began baptizing infants for the forgiveness of sin, separated themselves from this error. Water baptism and the new birth of salvation are distinct in Scripture and need to be kept distinct. There is no salvation in water baptism no matter how many insist otherwise. There is no washing away of sin, original or otherwise, with water no matter how

101

insistent Roman Catholicism is. Baptists have always insisted that water baptism is not a part of Salvation as explained in the Bible, and justly so. However, Catholics know the verses well "The like figure where unto *even* <u>baptism</u> doth also now save us" (1Pet 3:21) Their whole doctrine of salvation hinges on the water of baptism because the Bible says "Then Peter said unto them, Repent, and be <u>baptized</u> every one of you in the name of Jesus Christ for the remission of sins," (Acts 2:38) Although we know from Scripture that Salvation is not accomplished by baptism, and we know that there is no water that could wash a sin away, we will have to deal carefully with these two verses that seem to state otherwise. We do that with careful exegesis, always letting Scripture interpret Scripture. Such process is often called a hermeneutical spiral whereby we circle through all the Bible's content while we center in on a prevailing truth or principle.

So too, when we know the Bible is clear about the volition of man for the salvation of his soul, we will have to clarify some verses which seem to indicate otherwise. The important part, again, is that we get the system of doctrine correct and aligned with the preponderance of Scripture and not let a couple 'stray verses' sway the truth. The basis for Catholic doctrine is that their baptismal water washes sin away. It is in error. The basis for Presbyterian doctrine is that some unsaved, unregenerate souls are elected for salvation from the foundation of the world. It is in error. It is necessary to carefully examine those Scriptures that seem to support Calvinism and understand their context without stepping into Calvin's error of thinking that individual soul's are elect for salvation or chosen for destruction.

When the erroneous doctrine of election is adopted prior to Bible exegesis the errors begin to compound. Examine here the Scriptures used in Easton's Revised Bible Dictionary under 'Election of Grace' and then under 'Predestination' and notice the swift compounding of the error. They contend that since God decrees the destiny of individual souls, he must decree every detail of human life, every detail in the whole universe thereby gets erroneously placed in a decree of God.

Easton's Errors on Election of Grace He states:

E
R
R
O
R
E
R
R
O
R
E
R
R
O
R
E
R
R
O
R

" The Scripture speaks

1. of the election of individuals to office or to honour and privilege, e.g., Abraham, Jacob, Saul, David, Solomon, were all chosen by God for the positions they held; so also were the apostles.

2. There is also an election of nations to special privileges, e.g., the Hebrews # De 7:6 Rom 9:4

3. But in addition there is an election of individuals to eternal life #2Th 2:13 Eph 1:4 1Pet 1:2 John 13:18 The ground of this election to salvation is the good pleasure of God # Eph 1:5,11 Mt 11:25,26 John 15:16,19 God claims the right so to do # Rom 9:16,21 It is not conditioned on faith or repentance, but is of sovereign grace # Rom 11:4-6 Eph 1:3-6 All that pertain to salvation, the means # Eph 2:8 2Th 2:13 as well as the end, are of God # Acts 5:31 2Ti 2:25 1Co 1:30 Eph 2:5,10 Faith and repentance and all other graces are the exercises of a regenerated soul; and regeneration is God's work, a 'new creature.' Men are elected 'to salvation,' 'to the adoption of sons,' 'to be holy and without blame before him in love' #2Th 2:13 Ga 4:4,5 Eph 1:4 The ultimate end of election is the praise of God's grace # Eph 1:6,12"

Eaton's UnBiblical Error is Contended:

We have already examined each of these Scriptures to refute the election of individual souls for Salvation. Salvation must be based on obedience to God via mans free will and such a free will decision is available to all. The Calvinist carefully stacks the deck here, carefully avoiding the 'whosoever will' verses and twisting the verses on election to imply that they have something to do with how one gets saved. One gets saved by their free will acceptance of God's eternal Son. Once saved they are in an army of elect ones who are elect for a purpose and service in God's kingdom, not elected for a salvation experience.

Eaton's Errors on Predestination He states:

E
R
R
O
R
E
R
R
O
R
E
R

" This word is properly used only with reference to God's plan or purpose of salvation. The Greek word rendered 'predestinate' is found only in these six passages, # Acts 4:28 Rom 8:29,30 1Co 2:7 Eph 1:5,11 and in all of them it has the same meaning. They teach that the eternal, sovereign, immutable, and unconditional decree or 'determinate purpose' of God governs all events. This doctrine of predestination or election is beset with many difficulties. It belongs to the 'secret things' of God. But if we take the revealed word of God as our guide, we must accept this doctrine with all its mysteriousness, and settle all our questionings in the humble, devout acknowledgment, 'Even so, Father: for so it seemed good in thy sight.' For the teaching of Scripture on this subject let the following passages be examined in addition to those

ERROR E referred to above;

Ge 21:12 Ex 9:16 33:19 De 10:15 32:8 Jos 11:20 1Sa 12:22

#2Ch 6:6 Ps 33:12 65:4 78:68 135:4 Isa 41:1-10 Jer 1:5 Mr 13:20

Luk 22:22 John 6:37 15:16 17:2,6,9 Acts 2:28 3:18 4:28 Acts 13:48 17:26

Rom 9:11,18,21 11:5 Eph 3:11 1Th 1:4 2Th 2:13 2Ti 1:9 Ti 1:2 1Pet 1:2

Hodge has well remarked that, rightly understood, this doctrine

1. exalts the majesty and absolute sovereignty of God, while it illustrates the riches of his free grace and his just displeasure with sin.

2. It enforces upon us the essential truth that salvation is entirely of grace. That no one can either complain if passed over, or boast himself if saved.

3. It brings the inquirer to absolute self-despair and the cordial embrace of the free offer of Christ.

4. In the case of the believer who has the witness in himself, this doctrine at once deepens his humility and elevates his confidence to the full assurance of hope"

Eaton's UnBiblical Error is Contended:

Again notice the leap from Scripture as they gloss over theses 6 important verses and excuse them all as supporting their 'Decreeing All Things' 'sacred cow', when in context none of them make this undefended leap. They connect all of them to a man's personal salvation experience, when none address individual salvation. Their preconceived intention that God, in his sovereignty chose some for salvation and some for damnation over rides all honest examination of these Scriptures. Hodges 4 points puts exponential emphasis on 1) the sovereignty of God in his selection of who gets grace, 2) that God's grace is somehow exalted by His doing the choosing without the 'whosoever will' doing the choosing, 3) That election brings man to self despair rather than Christ's sermon on the mount bringing man to self despair, and lastly that 4) a misnomered doctrine of election is somehow humbling to those who are hand chosen to get 'in' as they repeat the phrase 'not by merit just by random selection!' No, indeed, their ill fated doctrine that God elected some to get in and some to get hell is unjust, ungodly and not-Scriptural no matter how much rhetoric they engage.

Easton's Errors on Decrees of God He states:

"The decrees of God are his eternal, unchangeable, holy, wise, and sovereign purpose, comprehending at once all things that ever were or will be in their causes, conditions, successions, and relations, and determining their certain futurition. The several contents of this one eternal purpose are, because of the limitation of our faculties, necessarily conceived of by us in partial aspects,

<table>
<tr><td>E
R
R
O
R

E
R
R
O
R

E
R
R
O
R

E
R
R
O
R

E
R
R
O
R</td><td>

and in logical relations, and are therefore styled Decrees." The decree being the act of an infinite, absolute, eternal, unchangeable, and sovereign Person, comprehending a plan including all his works of all kinds, great and small, from the beginning of creation to an unending eternity; ends as well as means, causes as well as effects, conditions and instrumentalities as well as the events which depend upon them, must be incomprehensible by the finite intellect of man. The decrees are:

1. eternal # Acts 15:18 Eph 1:4 2Th 2:13

2. unchangeable # Ps 33:11 Isa 46:9

3. comprehend all things that come to pass # Eph 1:11 Mt 10:29,30 # Eph 2:10 Acts 2:23 4:27,28 Ps 17:13,14

4. efficacious, as they respect those events he has determined to bring about by his own immediate agency; or

5. permissive, as they respect those events he has determined that free agents shall be permitted by him to effect. This doctrine ought to produce in our minds "humility, in view of the infinite greatness and sovereignty of God, and of the dependence of man; confidence and implicit reliance upon wisdom, righteousness, goodness, and immutability of God's purpose."
</td></tr>
</table>

Eaton's UnBiblical Error is Contended:

These decrees are fictitious. They are derived in the mind of the theologian and nowhere in the Scriptures of God. They imply fixity. God's revelation from Genesis to Revelation implies fluidity. They imply fatalism. God's word reveals dynamicism. They contend for the unchangeable. God's word in teaching us to pray contends that He can and will change things. They contend that the destiny of your soul is sealed before the foundation of the earth. God's word contends that "Whosoever Will" may come, and that the destiny of your soul is only sealed in two ways. First, it is sealed when you receive Christ as your eternal Lord and Saviour of your soul. He then seals your destiny and you become predestinated. Secondly when you draw your last breath in this life in rejection of the loving sacrifice of His dear Son, the Bible says your doom is sealed in that breath. "For God so loved the world, that he gave his only begotten Son, that whosoever believeth in him should not perish, but have everlasting life. For God sent not his Son into the world to condemn the world; but that the world through him might be saved. He that believeth on him is not condemned: **but he that believeth not is condemned already**, because he hath not believed in the name of the only begotten Son of God." (John 3:16-18) Herein there are but two ways one can seal his eternal fate. And herein God did not seal it. Man must in his free will as a free moral agent make his own choice. God has drawn on the heart or 'reins' of every man. God has called every man to repentance and salvation. Whether one moves his fingers left or right today is not something that was decreed before the foundation of the earth. The ludicrousness of such teaching and the rhetoric that is engaged to defend it is telling. God's plan for your life today is locked into nothing but fluidity. The opportunities for you to be conformed to the image of His dear Son loom before us each day. God has provided great opportunities, knows great possibilities, prepares great places for your service to him each day,... don't entertain a theology teaching that your choice to participate yeah or nay is locked up in his decree or even in his foreknowledge. Such is not borne out in Scripture.

We need to practice good Biblical exegesis on determining a doctrine of election and predestination, John Calvin and St. Agustine did not. Presbyterian and Reformed theologians do not. Baptists, as people of the book (that's the BIBLE not the reformed Augustinian theology book,) need to especially give this vile doctrine wide berth.

Chapter 12 The Dangers of Calvinistic Error

When man develops and defends an errant doctrine to such a degree that Calvinistic doctrine has been taken, you can guess two things about the error. First, it is an error that appeals to the natural heart of man. There is something in its core that appeals to the rebellion in man and thus it holds an attraction that causes it to catch on and grow and take on a life of its own. Second it is an error which draws away from the Cross of Calvary, its necessity, its totality its singular Gospel message, and God's election of Christians to be its witness to this world.

For example, the doctrine of religious works is also such an errant implant in the heart of man. The two errors stand in stark contrast that man must a) do everything necessary to attain heaven, and b) that man can do absolutely nothing to attain heaven, it is but ones destiny, i.e. God laid it all out before the foundation of the world. It is not in the Bible, that a man can do enough good in his life that he deserves to go to heaven, but such is the expectation of the religious masses. Catholic doctrine expands on the error with a system of doing sacraments, penance and indulgence to combat the mortal and venial sins that man does. The Protestants all propagate such a concept that at the pearly gates Peter will weigh in with our good and our bad as we wait and hope the scale tips to our favor. Even United Methodist doctrine (though protestant, they are called out here because they used to preach the saving gospel that the Wesley brothers founded) today says you must receive Christ 'and he will help you be good enough' to get in. "You can not get in without Jesus", they will say, "but Jesus does not save you, he just makes it possible for you to be good enough to get in." Such a doctrine of works salvation is a broad gate and wide path, and many there be that go in thereat.

Religion is attractive to our old nature of doing something for ourself and doing it religiously. So too is the Presbyterian doctrine of election and predestination attractive to our old nature that says "It is not my fault",... "it was the serpent that beguiled me,"... "it is the woman you gave me,"... "it is God's election that determines if a neighbor accepts Him, it is not my lazy witness, it is not my lost zeal, lost testimony, nor inept prayer life." Both of these errors are rooted deep, both form the wide gate of the majority, both are un-Scriptural, and both are filling the legions of hell with souls. Both need to be combated by Baptists who will contend for the faith. The former is battled on every Baptist front, but the latter has seeped into our Baptist circles and marinates our soul winning witness in lethargic laziness. The regular Baptists weigh in with 2, 2 ½, 3 or even 5 points of the error and think themselves justifiably scholarly and Scriptural. They will not cast out the Presbyterian reformed TULIP and resort to the pure Biblical doctrine, that your neighbor, your spouse, your loved one is a 'whosoever' and must make a decision for Christ themselves and that decision can possibly rest on your witness, your testimony, your walk, and your closet of prayer. In completely fleeing this error one would better hold to no predestination, no election, no selection before the foundation of the world; no hanging it on the way it was 'meant to be' in any kind of decree of God, nor foreknowledge of God, nor providence of God.

Fisk lists these "Ten ill effects of rigid Calvinistic thinking" with which this author whole heartedly agrees.

1. It deters a zealous Christian witness
2. It deprives Scripture of meaning.
3. It misses the scope of God's plan.
4. It opens the door to certain extremes.
5. It instills pride in its adherents.
6. It involves Philosophic of Sophistries
7. It undermines faith in God's Justice.
8. It makes God the author of sin.
9. It disavows human responsibility.
10. It questions God's love for the world.

"These ten points, then, are some of the leading considerations that show it *does* make a difference when full-fledged Calvinism is embraced, and they show why it should be respectfully resisted.

"Other objections to it have been raised, For example, some have pointed out that it evokes disharmony among God's people and disrupts fellowships.[90]

Yeah, the poisonous errors of Calvinism go much deeper than even that. They deprive us of reading literally the revelation of God, thus denying the theological understanding of the Almighty, and detracting from the intimacy that he desires with his saints. But yeah,

---

[90]   Fisk, Samuel, "Calvinistic Paths Retraced",pp 185-216

the harm goes farther.

Robert Ingersoll, credited as founder of Atheism in America, was born son to a Presbyterian preacher in the village of Dresden where I now pastor Good Samaritan Baptist Church. Of course I will not here recommend his book "How I Became an Agnostic", but in its pages you would find his testimony that the evangelist preaching in his fathers Presbyterian Church, who painted a vivid picture of hell from Luke 16, and reported that souls were elect to avoid it and souls were chosen to taste of it, caused him to reject the Bible completely, and eventually reject that there could even be such a God who would choose to send men to such a horrid place. Indeed his latter premise was correct, there is no such God, except in the bowels of the Calvinistic teaching engulfed by the Presbyterian Church. Robert Ingersoll left this distasteful unbiblical teaching and became a great statesman and spokesman. But he was a spokesman for the hell that he rejected and became the founder of the atheism movement in these United States of America.

False teachings in the Church itself can be credited for the founding of all our modern cults. Indeed the false teaching of souls predestined to eternal bliss or eternal torment by a supposed God of love randomly choosing, is the leading cause of false religions. At the turn of the century Joseph Smith rejected such, armed himself with his own book of Mormon, and became founder of Latter Day Saints. Charles Taze Russell rejected such, then rejected all Christianity, and the dieity of Christ himself, and founded the JW movement. Mary Baker Glover Eddy rejected such and founded the Christian Science movement. Ellen White rejected such and founded the Seven Day Adventists. Yeah indeed Satan has had a field day spinning off false teachers and founding false movements because of this very errant teaching that God ordained some to go to heaven and the rest to taste eternal destruction in the devil's hell. Indeed it does make a horrid difference when Calvinism is embraced, for it rejects the gospel message of the Bible!.

Again, God's "hand IS stretched out still" and "Whosoever therefore shall confess me before men,Mt 10:32, Lu 12:8" or "whosoever shall not be offended in me Mt 11:6, Lu 7:23" or "whosoever shall do the will of my Father which is in heaven, Mt 12:50, Mr 3:35" or "whosoever will save his life, Mt 16:25" or "Whosoever therefore shall humble himself, Mt 18:4" or "Whosoever will come after me, Mr 8:34" or "whosoever shall receive me, Mr 9:37, Lu 9:48" or

"Whosoever cometh to me, Lu 6:47" or "whosoever drinketh of the water that I shall give him, Joh 4:14" or "whosoever liveth and believeth in me Joh 11:26" or "through his name whosoever believeth in him Ac 10:43, Joh 3:15" or "whosoever believeth on him Ro 9:33, Ro 10:11" or " whosoever believeth on me Joh 12:46" or "whosoever shall call on the name of the Lord shall be saved. Rom 10:13" "For God so loved the world, that he gave his only begotten Son, that whosoever believeth in him should not perish, but have everlasting life." "For whosoever shall call upon the name of the Lord shall be saved." ... "That if thou shalt confess with thy mouth the Lord Jesus, and shalt believe in thine heart that God hath raised him from the dead, thou shalt be saved. For with the heart man believeth unto righteousness; and with the mouth confession is made unto salvation. For the scripture saith, Whosoever believeth on him shall not be ashamed."

Salvation is not for the elect, it is for the whosoever. "It is done. I am Alpha and Omega, the beginning and the end. I will give unto him that is athirst of the fountain of the water of life freely."(Rev 21:6)

Chapter 13 Romans Chapter 9, Election by God's Design

A marvelous understanding of election can be attained with the proper representation of Romans Chapter 9. This chapter fits compactly into Paul's larger argument of chapters 9 through 11 and this larger argument fits compactly into Paul's whole thesis written to the Romans, i.e. to Gentiles, i.e. to you and I today.   This chapter will examine the argument introduced in Rom 9 in the context of Roman's larger thesis. Referencing this chapter out of context has been a short fall of those who support an errant doctrine of Calvinistic election. They particularly like the reasoning that God loved Jacob and hated Esau, contending that God chose Jacob for salvation, and Esau for damnation. This is not true. Salvation is not in topic in this section. The emphasis one should pursue in Bible study is to always keep things in their greater context. This is especially important for Baptists, who for 1,978 years have based all their faith and practice on the Words of this book.[91]

First, lets consider the context of the book as it fits into the whole Bible. Paul explains his purpose in his introduction. Rom 1:16-17 says "For I am not ashamed of the gospel of Christ for it is the power of God unto salvation to every one that believeth; to the Jew first, and also to the Greek. For therein is the righteousness of God revealed from faith to faith: as it is written , The just shall live by faith." Three important aspects of this theme shows up in Chapter 9; the various considerations of the Jew and Greek, the righteousness of God in His provision of grace to all, and the involvement of faith without the law. Paul's theme here is

---

[91]   The idea that Luther, Zwingly, Calvin, Knox or any other Protestant 'spawned' any Baptists, AnaBaptist, Waldensians, Albigenses, Arnoldists, Henricians, Donatists, Paulicians, or Montanists, who long preceded any of these 'Protesters' to Catholicism, and represent the 1,978 year old perpetuity of Baptist doctrine, especially that of salvation by grace alone and certainly that of believers baptism by immersion and voluntarianism of salvation, ... is preposterous. When Luther, Zwingli, Calvin, and Knox finally made their protest against Catholicism and affirmed that salvation is by faith without works or indulgence, they got the grace of God into the proper perspective, ... the perspective that Baptists, by various names previous, had then been preaching for 1,400 years! But these 'protesters' never got the doctrine of baptism even close to the Biblical doctrine, and they continued killing Baptists with their powerful union of Church and state.

the righteousness of God, his thesis is that God can provide salvation to man without compromising His holy righteousness and these three ingredients, Jew vs Greek, Righteousness vs propitiation, and faith vs law, are reoccurring articles in each argument. These three then necessarily flow into chapter 9-11, in fact they are the emphasis of this portion of scripture.

Secondly we should examine the transition from Paul's proper point in this thesis to his theme in chapters 9-11. The transition in chapter 8 is actually the crescendo of his whole previous development. "*There is* therefore now no condemnation to them which are in Christ Jesus, who walk not after the flesh, but after the Spirit. " (Rom 8:1) Paul had previously developed points that: man is without excuse, Chap 1; the judgment of God is just and sure, chap 2; all are guilty (Jew or Gentile) and none righteous, chap 3a; God by forbearance and in righteousness provides a propitiation, chap 3b; such salvation is by grace through faith, chap 4; there are results of this justification, chap 5; there is a change because of one's justification, chap 6; there is a standing because of one's justification, chap7; and chapter 8 now stands to introduce the nature and presence of the Spirit in our life, with special emphasis on the proper walk in the spirit.

Romans chapter 8 thus concludes the result of our justification with coverage of how the Holy Spirit now functions in a 'non condemned', 'not under the law' believer. The transitioning thought that closes this chapter is that separation from the love of Christ can not happen, even though, for Paul, the Jews press with unbelievable persecutions. Chapter 9 now introduces the heaviness in Paul's heart that the Jews, who were given the law, possessed the promised seed, and were called the elect of God, are still found in condemnation. "How can this be?" is the subject of Romans 9-11. The examination is a parentheses in his thesis. The parentheses ends at chapter 12 which opens with "I beseech ye (saved Gentiles) therefore brethren by the mercies of God, that you ..." These transitions frame the context of Paul's whole argument in chapters 9-11.

Paul then begins this section with an emphasis on his seriousness and ergo the seriousness of the issue. Words of verse 1 and 2 could not better express his sincerity, his heaviness and sorrow. The issue in focus is that 'The elect are lost and that does not seem fair!' Look at the question addressed in verse 14 "Is there unrighteousness with God?" Read these chapters a few times and one will agree on the dilemma that 'the elect are lost and that don't seem fair!' The former was the heaviness of Paul's heart the latter the righteous truth dealt with in this section of Scripture.

Notice also that a Presbyterian, Calvinist or Reformed doctrine of election goes immediately contrary to Paul's dilemma in this context. The election that Paul addresses here is not one of their soul towards salvation or damnation, but one of their body towards service to him. Keep this distinction clear in this dissertation and Paul's marvelous clarity will be striking. If you take a Calvinist view into his debate here, Paul's arguments get muddier and muddier untill you end stuck in mire, with mud on Paul's face. Don't do that. Paul kept it simple we should too.

In verse 4, Paul amply describes these kinsmen of his who are elect but lost. "Who are Israelites; to whom *pertaineth* the adoption," (adoption, wherein one is chosen and accepted with all the rights of son ship when not a natural born child, so herein Israel not a natural born son of God was chosen and accepted as an adopted son of God.)

"to whom *pertaineth* ... the covenants" (covenants, wherein God made legal binding agreements to his chosen people Israel.)

"to whom *pertaineth* ... the giving of the law" (wherein God gave Israel His words, His law, His testimonies, His ways, His precepts, His statutes, His commandments, His righteous judgments, the octet worded in an acrostic octet in Psalm 119)

"to whom *pertaineth* .. the services of God" (wherein more than any other description it is seen that Israels election was for service, not for the saving or damning of individual souls for eternity.)

"to whom *pertaineth* ... the promises" (wherein over and above the adoption glory and the covenants , there are marvelous eternal promises given to Israel. Such promises will bring to pass the regathering and salvation of all Israel corporate, as detailed here in chapter 11:26-36 of Paul's coverage.)

This sevenfold description of the advantage in Israel concludes with: "Whose *are* the father, and of whom as concerning the flesh Christ came," (The crescendo of Paul's description centers here on the marvelous realization that these Israelites, who are lost to salvation by grace, who stumbled at Zion's cornerstone, were physically of the same fathers as was the Christ!) "who is over all , God blessed forever. Amen." (Paul very rarely writes the name of Christ without inserting praise and glory to his name.)

The word of God for Israel takes full effect only on a remnant of Jews. This rings equally true for man in this age of grace, but coming out from the age of law, the old covenant, this requires some analysis. The next 8 verses put some meat on the phrase "Many be called, but few chosen." Jesus used this phrase twice. In Matt 20:16 to crown a parable which included his statement "Is it not lawful for me to do what I will with my own? Is mine eye evil, because I am good?" Now this parable, proper was primarily intended to teach that the first shall be last and the last shall be first. The secondary emphasis is that God can do with his resources as he pleases, and this directly comes to bear on Romans 9.

The second use of Christ's statement "many are called, but few are chosen" is given in Matt 22:14. Here it is in reference to the man called into the wedding feast who "had not on a wedding garment" and was speechless for why not. He was cast out into outer darkness, and the crown of this thought is this profound statement of our study "For many are called, but few are chosen."

With this teaching as a backdrop look at Paul's heart for Israel portrayed in Romans 9. In verse 6 Paul says "Not as though the word of God hath taken none effect. For they are not all Israel, which are of Israel: Neither, because they are the seed of Abraham, are they all children: but In Isaac shall thy seed be called." The principle thought here is that the word of God does have an effect on some. The two points of emphasis are that not all the children of Abraham were the children of God, and not all the children of God were the chosen seed. Notice in this, and in verses 8-13, that there is given detail about this 'down sizing of specific promise, specific calling and specific service.

Paul explains that the word of God did have an effect... But "they *are* not all Israel, which are of Israel: ... (vrs 6) ... "That is, they which are the children of the flesh, these *are* not the children of God: but the children of the promise are counted for the seed. For this *is* the word of promise. 'At this time will I come and Sarah shall have a son'." (Paul directly referencing Gen 18:10 in verses Rom 9:8-9)

Paul further explains that the word of God did have an effect .... But "Neither, because they are the seed (proper) of Abraham *are they* all children: but 'In Isaac thy seed be called." (Paul directly referencing Gen 21:12, reading this as from within Isaac implying a further narrowing in selection in verse 7) ... "but when Rebecca also conceived by one, *even* by our father Isaac; ... It was said unto her, 'The elder shall serve the younger" (Paul directly referencing Genesis 25:23) ... "As it is written, 'Jacob have I loved, but Esau have I hated:'" (Paul directly referencing Malachi 1:2-3) Herein Paul illustrates the effect that the word of God did have. It did not effect all that we might expect, but God had his purposes and his eye on an unfolding plan that He was bringing to pass.

Paul adds a formidable parenthetical explanation to this reasoning to emphasize that the purpose of God is the main driver for considering God's election for service. He adds "For *the children* being not yet born, neither having done any good or evil, that the purpose of God according to election might stand, not of works, but of him that calleth;)"

For our purpose of clarification we will point out again that election is for the purpose of service to God and not for salvation. Esau was hated as the chromosomes donor for the seed, but such had no bearing on whether he believed God or not, whether he was counted righteous or not, saved or lost. This was a DNA selection for the seed of Messiah. Did this despise have an adverse effect on Esau and Edom? Well, did God's despise for Cain's offering have an effect on Cain and his line? Certainly God's election of some for specific service has an effect on the directions of people and generations. This reasoning leads to Paul's next question found in Rom 9:14.

"What shall we say then? *Is there* unrighteousness with God? God forbid." Revisit Paul's dilemma again, 'It does not seem fair that God's Elect, Israel, should go predominately unsaved.' Indeed now his declaration rings more clear "*Is there* unrighteousness with God? God forbid." This wrestling has nothing to do with an election towards salvation His argument continues and is more pointed in verse 15 and 16. "For he saith to Moses, I will have mercy on whom I will have mercy, and I will have compassion on whom I will have compassion. [16] So then *it is* not of him that willeth, nor of him that runneth, but of God that sheweth mercy." Again keep in focus what Paul is wrestling with as you examine each argument.

Next Paul examines the Pharaoh who hardened his heart against letting Israel go from Egypt. Note particularly here that God's purpose in raising up a Pharaoh who would harden his heart, was not for the condemnation of his soul, but for the pursuit of a contest between God and king. As it says "that I might shew my power in thee, and that my name might be declared throughout all the earth." (Rom 9:17b) Again, God's election is not for eternal salvation or damnation but for God's purposes here in this life, on this side of eternity.

In verse 19 Paul takes an interesting track. He anticipates a question from a reader and promptly cut's it off. Verse 19; " Thou wilt say then unto me, Why doth he yet find fault? For who hath resisted his will?" With the readers questioning anticipated Paul now develops his argument of verse 20-24 for the potter creating the clay anyway he pleases. It begins thus:

20 Nay but, O man, who art thou that repliest against God? Shall the thing formed say to him that formed *it*, Why hast thou made me thus?"

Notice that the portion of this argument which justifies God making some "vessels of wrath fitted for destruction" is guarded with the clause "*What if* God,..." This is not presented as how God did operate, but instead it is presented as how God could have justifiably operated.

With the fairness issue well put to bed, Paul turns his attention to the marvelous acceptance of the Gentiles for this call to salvation. Remember again that Paul's original dilemma was that the elect Jews were perishing without Christ. In verses 24 through the end of the chapter this inclusion of Gentiles for salvation, and the exclusion of Jews for salvation is carefully detailed with Scripture references. The Jews were not included because they stumbled at the stumblingstone, not because they missed an election. The Gentiles were included for the call to salvation because Christ said "Whosoever will may come," and not because they got a special election for their souls. If the Reformed Augustinian doctrine that certain souls were chosen before the foundation of the world, elected to receive saving grace, and other souls were not chosen and must go without this grace; ... if such a doctrine were true then Paul would be demonstrating gross negligence in not spelling it out in this portion of Scripture. If the Jews went unsaved simply because God had not so chosen them for a salvation experience, then Paul would most certainly have declared such a doctrine in Romans chapter 9. He does not. In fact, going in with such an ill conceived assumption muddies this chapter beyond clarification. Paul is not a muddy communicator. His argument justifying a majority of God's elect but stiff necked nation, Israel, missing out on salvation, does not support any conception of individual souls elect before the foundation of the world. So don't muddy the water in Romans chapter 9.

Chapter 14 Conclusion

The gross error of the 5 point Calvinistic model of election for salvation has long been realized by Baptists and other Bible believers. As a Roman Catholic holds on to their religious works and sacraments for salvation because it appeals to their fallen nature of a making ones own righteousness, so the Calvinist holds on to their 'its all in God's hands' mentality because it appeals to their fallen nature of 'its not my fault', blame God. Baptists, with a long bloody history of believing what the Bible literally says, have spent the last few years word smithing this erroneous doctrine of election to try and feed that fallen nature. Today, Regular Baptists have a degree of acceptance of this erroneous doctrine, as they choose out whether they are one, two, two and a half, or three point Calvinists. Southern Baptist have even started to embrace the Presbyterian error of Calvinistic teaching on election. Shame on any Baptists for this poisonous compromise. Independent Baptists have included this fatalistic doctrine by word smithing with God's foreknowledge. We say such treachery as "God, knows from the foundation of the earth who will get saved and who will get damned, ... but he doesn't elect them as such." That is word smithing balderdash.

Souls are neither slated for an eternity by election, nor slated for an eternity by foreknowledge, every soul is given a call and a choice. The Bible is clear, eternal heaven or eternal hell hangs on a volitional choice of each individual. It says "And the Spirit and the bride say, Come. And let him that heareth say, Come. And let him that is athirst come. And whosoever will, let him take the water of life freely." (Rev 22:17)

The poison of this heretical doctrine of election has infiltrated Christian ranks like lead from the early food canning processes slowly accumulated in recipients. Like lead poisoning, it has a hidden but devastating effects and it takes both recognition and a long process of purging to attain a recovery. Reread this Biblical doctrine of election and predestination. Then reread your Holy Bible, Genesis to Revelation. Avoid the old, early canned foods. And may the LORD bless you in a quest to pray a soul out of hell and into heaven Prayer changes things. And may the LORD bless you with a witness for Christ, not because of duty but because of its effect on souls. And may the LORD bless you with a desire to pick up that poor neighbor's children and get them to Church, perhaps in a Baptist Sunday School bus that used to run before the Calvinistic error crept in.

If you are a Pastor, Bible School graduate, or Seminary Graduate who has read this book, please send it to your old Bible Doctrine professor, or soteriology professor. The truthful Biblical Doctrine of Election and Predestination needs to be disseminated.

Glossary

an·tin·o·my (ăn-tĭn′ə-mē) *n., pl.* **an·tin·o·mies**. **1.** Contradiction or opposition, especially between two laws or rules. **2.** A contradiction between principles or conclusions that seem equally necessary and reasonable; a paradox. [Latin *antinomia,* from Greek : *anti-,* anti- + *nomos,* law; see **nem-** below.] **--an′ti·nom′ic** (ăn′tĭ-nŏm′ĭk) *adj.*

a·o·rist (ā′ər-ĭst) *Grammar. n. Abbr.* **aor. 1.** A form of a verb in some languages, such as Classical Greek, that expresses action without indicating its completion or continuation. **2.** A form of a verb in some languages, such as Classical Greek or Sanskrit, that in the indicative mood expresses past action. [From Greek *aoristos,* indefinite, aorist tense : *a-,* not; see *horistos,* definable (from *horizein,* to define; see HORIZON).] **--a′o·ris′tic** *adj.* **--a′o·ris′ti·cal·ly** *adv.*

ar·ti·cle (är′tĭ-kəl) *n. Abbr.* **art. 1.** ... **2.** A particular section or item of a series in a written document, as in a contract, constitution, or treaty. **3.** A nonfictional literary composition that forms an independent part of a publication, as of a newspaper or magazine.

au·thor·i·tar·i·an (ə-thôr′ĭ-târ′ē-ən, ə-thŏr′-, ô-thôr′-, ô-thŏr′-) *adj.* **1.** Characterized by or favoring absolute obedience to authority, as against individual freedom: *an authoritarian regime.* **2.** Of, relating to, or expecting unquestioning obedience. See Synonyms at **dictatorial. --au·thor′i·tar′i·an** *n.* **-- au·thor′i·tar′i·an·ism** *n.*

bi·as (bī′əs) *n.* **1.** ... **2.** *Usage Problem.* **a.** A preference or an inclination, especially one that inhibits impartial judgment. **b.** An unfair act or policy stemming from prejudice. **3.** A statistical sampling or testing error caused by systematically favoring some outcomes over others. ... **--bi·as** *adj.* **1.** Slanting or diagonal; oblique: *a bias fold.* **--bi·as** *tr.v.* **bi·ased** or **bi·assed, bi·as·ing** or **bi·as·sing, bi·as·es** or **bi·as·ses. 1.** To influence in a particular, typically unfair direction; prejudice. **2.** ... [French *biais,* slant, from Provençal, perhaps ultimately from Greek *epikarsios,* slanted.]

Chris·tian (krĭs′chən) *adj.* **1.** Professing belief in Jesus as Christ or following the religion based on the life and teachings of Jesus. **2.** Relating to or derived from Jesus or Jesus's teachings. **3.** Manifesting the qualities or spirit of Jesus; Christlike. **4.** Relating to or characteristic of Christianity or its adherents. **5.** Showing a loving concern for others; humane. **--Chris·tian** *n. Abbr.* **Chr. 1.** One who professes belief in Jesus as Christ or follows the religion based on the life and teachings of Jesus. **2.** One who lives according to the teachings of Jesus. [Middle English *Cristen,* from Old English *cristen,* from Latin *Christiānus,* from Greek *Khristianos,* from *Khristos,* Christ. See CHRIST.] **--Chris′tian·ly** *adj. & adv.*

WORD HISTORY (by Pastor Edward Rice): A Christian by original and stricter definition is one who is Christlike in behavior because he has previously become a believer in Christ and been trained as a disciple of Christ. The first use of the word was not just to believers but to disciples in The Acts of the Apostles chapter 11, verse 26 it says *"And the disciples were called Christians first in Antioch."* To be a believer in Christ one must affirm Jesus Christ as God and saviour of their soul. Thus cults, which deny the trinity of the Godhead and Deity of the Lord Jesus Christ are not Christian. Fundamental Christians are those who go back to the fundamentals of the Biblical teachings of Christ as the source of all faith and practice. Thus the religion of Roman Catholicism, a religion which unites Church and State, a religion which mandates and forces the baptism into their ranks (by mandatory infant baptism, by law and even by sword, see their doctrine of two swords), a religion which utilizes Roman celibate priests and buying and selling of penance, (this due to their Latin mistranslation of the term 'presbyter' to priest and the term 'repentance' to penance), a religion which holds a Pope as their infallible authority and not the Bible, is not Christian. And the protestant daughters of the Roman religion who strove to burn and drown Christians with such a uniting of Church and State powers, and still Baptize their infants (infant Baptism is a Roman practice nowhere sanctioned in the Bible) are not Christian in practice but Roman.

de·cree (dǐ-krē′) *n.* **1.** An authoritative order having the force of law. **2.** *Law.* The judgment of a court of equity, admiralty, probate, or divorce. **3.** *Roman Catholic Church.* **a.** A doctrinal or disciplinary act of an ecumenical council. **b.** An administrative act applying or interpreting articles of canon law. **--de·cree** *v.* **de·creed, de·cree·ing, de·crees.** *--tr.* **1.** To ordain, establish, or decide by decree. See Synonyms at **dictate.** *--intr.* To issue a decree. [Middle English *decre*, from Old French *decret*, from Latin *dēcrētum*, principle, decision, from neuter past participle of *dēcernere*, to decide : *dē-*, de- + *cernere*, to sift; see **krei-** below.] **--de·cree′a·ble** *adj.* **--de·cre′er** *n.*

dis·in·gen·u·ous (dǐs′ǐn-jěn′yōō-əs) *adj.* Not straightforward or candid; crafty: *"an ambitious, disingenuous, philistine, and hypocritical operator, who . . . exemplified . . . the most disagreeable traits of his time"* (David Cannadine).

e·lect (ǐ-lěkt′) *v.* **e·lect·ed, e·lect·ing, e·lects.** *--tr.* **1.** To select by vote for an office or for membership. **2.** To pick out; select: *elect an art course.* See Synonyms at **choose. 3.** To decide, especially by preference: *elected to take the summer off.* **4.** *Theology.* To select by divine will for salvation. *--intr.* **1.** To make a choice or selection. **--e·lect** *adj.* **1.** Chosen deliberately; singled out. **2.a.** Elected but not yet installed. Often used in combination: *the governor-elect.* **b.** Chosen for marriage. Often used in combination: *the bride-elect.* **3.** *Theology.* Selected by divine will for salvation. **--e·lect** *n.* **1.** One that is chosen or selected. **2.** *Theology.* One selected by divine will for salvation. **3.** (used with a pl. verb). An exclusive group of people. Used with *the*: *one of the elect who have power inside the government.* [Middle English *electen*, from Latin *ēligere*, ēlēct-, to select : *ē-, ex-*, ex- + *legere*, to choose; see **leg-** below.]

e·lec·tion (ǐ-lěk′shən) *n.* **1.a.** The act or power of electing. **b.** The fact of being elected. **2.** The right or ability to make a choice. See Synonyms at **choice. 3.** *Theology.* Predestined salvation, especially as conceived by Calvinists.

e·van·gel·ism (ǐ-văn′jə-lǐz′əm) *n.* **1.** Zealous preaching and dissemination of the gospel, as through missionary work. **2.** Militant zeal for a cause. **--e·van′gel·is′tic** (-jə-lǐs′tǐk) *adj.* **--e·van′gel·is′ti·cal·ly** *adv.*

e·van·gel·ize (ǐ-văn′jə-līz′) *v.* **e·van·gel·ized, e·van·gel·iz·ing,**

e·van·gel·iz·es. *--tr.* **1.** To preach the gospel to. **2.** To convert to Christianity. -- *intr.* To preach the gospel. **--e·van′gel·i·za′tion** (-jə-lĭ-zā′shən) *n.* -- **e·van′gel·iz′er** *n.*

    ex·e·ge·sis (ĕk′sə-jē′sĭs) *n., pl.* **ex·e·ge·ses** (-sēz). Critical explanation or analysis, especially of a text. [Greek *exēgēsis,* from *exēgeisthai,* to interpret : *ex-,* ex- + *hēgeisthai,* to lead; see **sāg-** below.] **sāg-.** Important derivatives are: *seek, sake, forsake, ransack, presage, sagacious, hegemony.* **sāg-.** To seek out. Contracted from **saag-.* **1.** Suffixed form **sāg-yo-.* SEEK, from Old English *sǣcan, sēcan,* to seek, from Germanic **sōkjan.* **2.** Suffixed form **sāg-ni-.* SOKE, from Old English *sōcn,* attack, inquiry, right of local jurisdiction, from Germanic **sōkniz.* **3.** Zero-grade form **səg-.* **a.** SAKE, from Old English *sacu,* lawsuit, case, from Germanic derivative noun **sakō,* "a seeking," accusation, strife; **b.** *(i)* FORSAKE, from Old English *forsacan,* to renounce, refuse (*for-,* prefix denoting exclusion or rejection; see **per**); *(ii)* RANSACK, from Old Norse **saka,* to seek. Both *(i)* and *(ii)* from Germanic **sakan,* to seek, accuse, quarrel. Both **a** and **b** from Germanic **sak-.* **4.** Independent suffixed form **sāg-yo-.* PRESAGE, from Latin *sāgīre,* to perceive, "seek to know." **5.** Zero-grade form **səg-.* SAGACIOUS, from Latin *sagāx,* of keen perception. **6.** Suffixed form **sāg-eyo-.* EXEGESIS, HEGEMONY, from Greek *hēgeisthai,* to lead (< "to track down"). [Pokorny *sāg-* 876.]

    mor·tal (môr′tl) *adj.* **1.** Liable or subject to death. **2.** Of or relating to humankind; human: *the mortal limits of understanding.* **3.** Of, relating to, or accompanying death: *mortal throes.* **4.** Causing death; fatal: *a mortal wound.* See Synonyms at **fatal. 5.** Fighting or fought to the death; unrelenting: *a mortal enemy; a mortal attack.* **6.** Of great intensity or severity; dire: *mortal terror.* **7.** Conceivable: *no mortal reason for us to go.* **8.** Used as an intensive: *a mortal fool.* **--mor·tal** *n.* A human being. [Middle English, from Old French, from Latin *mortālis,* from *mors,* mort-, death. See **mer-** below.] **--mor′tal·ly** *adv.*

    or·dain (ôr-dān′) tr.v. **or·dained, or·dain·ing, or·dains. 1.a.** *To invest with ministerial or priestly authority; confer holy orders on.* **b.** *To authorize as a rabbi.* **2.** *To order by virtue of superior authority; decree or enact.* **3.** *To prearrange unalterably; predestine: by fate ordained. See Synonyms at* **dictate.** *[Middle English ordeinen, from Old French ordener, ordein-, from Latin ōrdināre, to organize, appoint to office, from ōrdō, ōrdin-, order. See* **ar-** *below.]* **--or·dain′er** *n.* **--or·dain′ment** *n.*

    pre·des·ti·nate (prē-dĕs′tə-nāt′) tr.v. **pre·des·ti·nat·ed, pre·des·ti·nat·ing, pre·des·ti·nates. 1.** *Theology. To predestine.* **2.** *Archaic. To destine or determine in advance; foreordain.* **--pre·des·ti·nate** *(-nĭt, -nāt′) adj. Foreordained; predestined. [Middle English predestinaten, from Late Latin praedēstināre, praedēstināt-. See PREDESTINE.]*

    pre·des·tine (prē-dĕs′tĭn) tr.v. **pre·des·tined, pre·des·tin·ing, pre·des·tines. 1.** *To fix upon, decide, or decree in advance; foreordain.* **2.** *Theology. To foreordain or elect by divine will or decree. [Middle English predestinen, from Old French predestiner, from Late Latin praedēstināre : Latin* *prae-, pre- + Latin dēstināre, to determine; see DESTINE.]*

pre·text *(prē′tĕkst′) n.* **1.** *An ostensible or professed purpose; an excuse.* **2.** *An effort or a strategy intended to conceal something.* **--pre·text** *tr.v.* **pre·text·ed**, **pre·text·ing**, **pre·texts**. *To allege as an excuse. [Latin praetextum, from neuter past participle of praetexere, to disguise : prae-, pre- + texere, to weave; see **teks-** below.]*

tran·scen·dent *(trăn-sĕn′dənt) adj.* **1.** *Surpassing others; preeminent or supreme.* **2.** *Lying beyond the ordinary range of perception: "fails to achieve a transcendent significance in suffering and squalor" (National Review).* **3.** *Philosophy.* **a.** *Transcending the Aristotelian categories.* **b.** *In Kant's theory of knowledge, being beyond the limits of experience and hence unknowable.* **4.** *Being above and independent of the material universe. Used of the Deity.* **-- tran·scen′dence** *or* **tran·scen′den·cy** *n.* **--tran·scen′dent·ly** *adv.*

trea·tise (trē′tĭs) *n.* **1.** A systematic, usually extensive written discourse on a subject. **2.** *Obsolete.* A tale or narrative. [Middle English *treatis*, from Anglo-Norman *tretiz*, alteration of *treteiz*, from Vulgar Latin **trāctātīcius*, from Latin *trāctātus*, past participle of *trāctāre*, to drag about, deal with. See TREAT.]

ve·ni·al (vē′nē-əl, vēn′yəl) *adj.* **1.** Easily excused or forgiven; pardonable: *a venial offense.* **2.** *Roman Catholic Church.* Minor, therefore warranting only temporal punishment. [Middle English, from Old French, from Late Latin *veniālis*, from Latin *venia*, forgiveness.] **--ve′ni·al′i·ty** (vē′nē-ăl′ĭ-tē, vēn-yăl′-) or **ve′ni·al·ness** (vē′nē-əl-nĭs, vēn′yəl-) *n.* **--ve′ni·al·ly** *adv.*

Appendix: Helpful Devotionals on Election

"My Utmost for His Highest" Oct 28ᵗʰ By Oswald Chambers
JUSTIFICATION BY FAITH

"For if, when we were enemies, we were reconciled to God by the death of His Son, much more, being reconciled, we shall be saved by His life." Rom 5:10

I am not saved by believing; I realize I am saved by believing. It is not repentance that saves me, repentance is the sign that I realize what God has done in Christ Jesus. The danger is to put the emphasis on the effect instead of on the cause. It is my obedience that puts me right with God, my consecration. Never! I am put right with God because prior to all, Christ died. When I turn to God and by belief accept what God reveals I can accept, instantly the stupendous Atonement of Jesus Christ rushes me into a right relationship with God; and by the supernatural miracle of God's grace I stand justified, not because I am sorry for my sin, not because I have repented, but because of what Jesus has done. The Spirit of God brings it with a breaking, all-over light, and I know, though I do not know how, that I am saved.

The salvation of God does not stand on human logic, it stands on the sacrificial Death of Jesus. We can be born again because of the Atonement of Our Lord. Sinful men and women can be changed into new creatures, not by their repentance or their belief, but by the marvelous work of God in Christ Jesus which is prior to all experience. The impregnable safety of justification and sanctification is God Himself. We have not to work out these things ourselves; they have been worked out by the Atonement. The supernatural becomes natural by the miracle of God; there is the realization of what Jesus Christ has already done - "It is finished."

C.H. Spurgeon's Morning Devotional
Sunday December 5, 2004 *"Ask, and it shall be given you."-Matthew 7:7*

We know of a place in England still existing, where a dole of bread is served to every passerby who chooses to ask for it. Whoever the traveller may be, he has but to knock at the door of St. Cross Hospital, and there is the dole of bread for him. Jesus Christ so loveth sinners that He has built a St. Cross Hospital, so that whenever a sinner is hungry, he has but to knock and have his wants supplied. Nay, He has done better; He has attached to this Hospital of the Cross a bath; and whenever a soul is black and filthy, it has but to go there and be washed. The fountain is always full, always efficacious. No sinner ever went into it and found that it could not wash away his stains. Sins which were scarlet and crimson have all disappeared, and the sinner has been whiter than snow. As if this were not enough, there is attached to this Hospital of the Cross a wardrobe, and a sinner making application simply as a sinner, may be clothed from head to foot; and if he wishes to be a soldier, he may not merely have a garment for ordinary wear, but armour which shall cover him from the sole of his foot to the crown of his head. If he asks for a sword, he shall have that given to him, and a shield too. Nothing that is good for him shall be denied him. He shall have spending-money so long as he lives, and he shall have an eternal heritage of glorious treasure when he enters into the joy of his Lord.

123

If all these things are to be had by merely knocking at mercy's door, O my soul, knock hard this morning, and ask large things of thy generous Lord. Leave not the throne of grace till all thy wants have been spread before the Lord, and until by faith thou hast a comfortable prospect that they shall be all supplied. No bashfulness need retard when Jesus invites. No unbelief should hinder when Jesus promises. No cold-heartedness should restrain when such blessings are to be obtained.

"My Utmost for His Highest" Jan 14th By Oswald Chambers

Called By God

I heard the voice of the Lord, saying: 'Whom shall I send, and who will go for Us?' Then I said, 'Here am I! Send me' —Isaiah 6:8

God did not direct His call to Isaiah—Isaiah overheard God saying, ". . . who will go for Us?" The call of God is not just for a select few but for everyone. Whether I hear God's call or not depends on the condition of my ears, and exactly what I hear depends upon my spiritual attitude. "*Many are called, but few are chosen*" (Matthew 22:14). That is, few prove that they are the chosen ones. The chosen ones are those who have come into a relationship with God through Jesus Christ and have had their spiritual condition changed and their ears opened. Then they hear "the voice of the Lord" continually asking, ". . . who will go for Us?" However, God doesn't single out someone and say, "Now, you go." He did not force His will on Isaiah. Isaiah was in the presence of God, and he overheard the call. His response, performed in complete freedom, could only be to say, "Here am I! Send me." Remove the thought from your mind of expecting God to come to force you or to plead with you. When our Lord called His disciples, He did it without irresistible pressure from the outside. The quiet, yet passionate, insistence of His "Follow Me" was spoken to men whose every sense was receptive (Matthew 4:19). If we will allow the Holy Spirit to bring us face to face with God, we too will hear what Isaiah heard-"the voice of the Lord." In perfect freedom we too will say, "Here am I! Send me."

Appendix: The Errant Doctrine Defined in Tulip

Total Depravity
Unconditional Election
Limited Atonement
Irresistible Grace
Perseverance of the Saints

! Total Depravity
Total depravity does not mean that every man is as bad as he could be or that no unredeemed man can do any good deed or honorable act. *Depravity* addresses man's spiritually dead condition because of the fall. *Total* addresses the fact that man's depravity has affected every area of his life and person. 4

! Unconditional Election
God's choice of who to save was made in eternity past and was not conditioned upon man's ability, life or future response to God's gracious offer of salvation.

! Limited Atonement
Sometimes called *Particular Redemption*, the subjects of Christ's atoning work on the cross are identified as only the elect. Jesus did not die for all the world. "God purposed by the atonement to save only the elect and that consequently all the elect, and they alone, are saved." R.B. Kuiper, "For Whom Did Christ Die?", p. 62

! Irresistible Grace
Sometimes called *Effective Grace*, addresses the belief that the Holy Spirit actually brings to salvation all the elect.

! Perseverance of the Saints
The security of the elect is guaranteed by God's power.

Appendix: Initial Research and Correspondence

10/20/2004
Dear Dr. Sproul,

I have been listening to your broadcast on Calvinism and am praying that you continue your struggle through this topic until you arrive at the truth that Jesus died for all of us, i.e. died for 'whosoever' will receive him, that God can save anybody, and that God is not willing that any should perish. As you freely confuse and intermix corporate election and individual soul election the struggle you are having with God seeming capricious is animated in this series. That is unfortunate for you and your listeners. As you endeavor to explain and defend Augustinian's gross error in Soteriology my prayer is that you and your audience will see your animated wrestling match with the truth. Individual souls were not predestined before the foundation of the earth, *mankind* was! More particularly Gentiles, corporately, like those in Ephesus were predestined and elect. My Bible says that Christ died for all, my Bible shows that God made man in his image with his own individual sovereignty, and my Bible says that God is not willing that any should perish. My Bible clearly departs from Augustinian's theory of soteriology. Don't miss these departures in your current study, I can't wait to hear from you which is right, my Bible or Calvin's TULIP. When you stay on the subject of what the Bible teaches I enjoy your lessons on WMHR in Syracuse immensely. When you go and paint yourself into the Reformed corners of Augustinian theory I feel bad for you. God is not capricious, there is a sovereignty of man and your gonna have wet paint on your feet and a mucked up paint job on your broadcast.

May God Bless you as you struggle with this truth, and may God make crystal clear His 'whosoever' truth despite the muddy water in your current broadcast.
In Christ

Pastor Ed Rice, Good Samaritan Baptist Church, Dresden NY.
REF: Chosen by God By RC Sproul www.ligonier.org
Paperback , 213 pages

* * * * * * *

From a Independent Baptist Sunday School Teacher   12/17/05
Dear Pastor Rice

I just wanted to drop you a line thanking you for your studies and writings on various topics. Sometimes we are not aware of the results or consequences of the things we do for the Lord.

The latest of these writings i have studied is your 'The Biblical Doctrine of Election and Predestination'. Pastor has given me the task of teaching a Sunday School series on "Predestination and Election". During the past weeks, i have read countless writings and studies and articles regarding this subject. I saved your writing for last in my research. By the time i got to the end, my mind was awash with confusion and i was on "verse overload"......

My goal is to teach this with scripture, clearly and simply as possible. Your booklet has squared me right with the Word of God and presented the truth in a clear manner.

126

Thank you for your study, work and devotion to the truth. I learned things i thought i knew were wrong. God's word is clear, and sometimes He needs to use faithful men to spray our brains with some "windex".

I intend to use a large portion of this booklet to teach this series.

Thanks for being a "window cleaner" for the Lord!

Adult Sunday School Teacher

* * * * * * *

Greetings Ed,   3 /04 /06

You come across as if you believe that finally, after 2,000 years, you have understood what nobody else ever has. I think you would do well to back up a bit on this strange new idea that God's omniscience only pertains to real time. To overcome an extreme position on election and predestination, is seems to me that you have gone to an extreme of your own.

God Bless,

Pastor ...Community Baptist Church

Mike,

Thanks, for the comment and concern. You are right on both counts, but I am extremely comfortable out here on this extreme but not extremely new position. I find it very Biblically based as well. You? If you would move out here just a little and step a bit further away from Calvinism (with your Bible open for sure) I'd be delighted. Just consider what the Bible actually says about omniscience as you read it through this year and I think you'll be more comfortable edging toward my 'extreme.' If not, let me know, I respect your opinion. If I get nervous out here and find Scriptures that make me so this year, I will recant. So far, 2 years in, I like it.

In God's Grace.

Ed Rice

Good Samaritan Baptist Church

www.GSBaptistChurch.com PastorRice@GSBaptistChurch.com

Index

Index of Scriptures and Terms

Bibliography

The Holy Bible

Anderson, Sir Robert, *"The Bible Or The Church"*, 2nd ed., London: Pickering and Inglis, n.d.

Augustine of Hippo, *"The Writings Against the Manichaeans and Against the Donatists"*, NPNF1-04 Edited by Philip Schaff (1819-1893) Eerdmans Publishing Company and published on the internett by The Library at Calvin College at www.ccel.org, Internet, Accessed Aug 2007.

_____ *"Letter to Donatus"*, No. 173 as printed in *"Select Library of Nicene and Post Nicene Fathers"*, ed, Philip Schaff, Vol. 1., Internet, accessed Aug 2007.

Allen, *"Religious Progress"*

Chambers, Oswald, *"My Utmost For His Highest"*

Dabney, R. L., *"The Five Points of Calvinism"*

Erickson, Millard J., *Christian Theology*

Fisk, Samuel, *"Calvinistic Paths Retraced"*, Printed by Biblical Evangelism Press @1985 ISBN 0-914012-25-8

Freeman, Paul L., *"What's Wrong With Five Point Calvinism"*

Ingersol, Robert, *"How I Became an Agnostic"*

Keyer, L.S. Dr., *"The Philosophy of Christianity"*

Kuiper, R.B. *"For whom Did Christ Die? "*

Rice, Richard, Sanders, John, *"The Openness of God: A Biblical Challenge to the Traditional Understanding of God"* (Paperback), Clark H. Pinnock (Editor), William Hasker (Contributor)

Richardson, Dr. Alan, *"An Introduction To The Theology Of The New Testament"*

Sanders, Dr. John, Article, http://www.opentheism.info accessed Feb 2007

Skeats, Herbert S., English historian (1688-1891), *"History of the Free Churches of England"*, (Unknown Binding - 1891)

Spurgeon, Charles Haddon, *"A Defense of Calvinism"* http://www.spurgeon.org/calvinis.htm, Internet, Accessed Aug 2007

Stevens, George B., *"The Theology of the New Testament"*

Stringer, Phil, Dr., *"The Faithful Baptist Witness"*, Landmark Baptist Press, 1998

Strong, Augustus H., *"Systematic Theology"*

Strong, James J. S.T.D., L.L.D., *"The Exhaustive Concordance of the Bible: Showing Every Word of the Test of the Common English Version of the Canonical Books"*

Telford, Andrew, *"Subjects of Sovereignty"*

Verduin, Leonard, *"The Reformers and Their Stepchildren"* Grand Rapids Wm. B. Eerdmans Pub. Co. @1964

Vincent, Marvin R., *"Word Studies in the New Testament "*

Waite, D.A., Th.D., Ph.D., *"The Case for the King James Bible"*, The Bible for today Press, @ 1998,2001 ISBN #1-56848-011-3

Warfield, Benjamin B., *"The Plan of Salvation"*

www.ingramcontent.com/pod-product-compliance
Lightning Source LLC
Chambersburg PA
CBHW032103080426
42733CB00006B/399